# CAMBRIDGE GREEK AND LATIN CLASSICS

GENERAL EDITORS

E. J. KENNEY

*Emeritus Kennedy Professor of Latin, University of Cambridge*

AND

P. E. EASTERLING

*Regius Professor of Greek, University of Cambridge*

D1471818

# VIRGIL
# AENEID
## BOOK XI

### EDITED BY
### K. W. GRANSDEN

*Emeritus Reader in English and Comparative Literary Studies,
University of Warwick*

CAMBRIDGE
UNIVERSITY PRESS

Published by the Press Syndicate of the University of Cambridge
The Pitt Building, Trumpington Street, Cambridge CB2 1RP
40 West 20th Street, New York, NY 10011–4211, USA
10 Stamford Road, Oakleigh, Melbourne 3166, Australia

First published 1991
Reprinted 1997

Printed in Great Britain at the University Press, Cambridge

*British Library cataloguing in publication data*

Virgil
[Aeneid. Book XI] Aeneid, Book XI – (Cambridge Greek and Latin classics)
I. [Aeneid. Book XI] II. Title III. Gransden, K. W.
(Karl Watts)
873.01

*Library of Congress cataloguing in publication data*

Virgil.
[Aeneis. Liber 11]
Aeneid, book XI / edited by K. W. Gransden.
p.    cm. – (Cambridge Greek and Latin classics)
Latin text: commentary in English.
Includes bibliographical references (p. 145) and indexes.
ISBN 0 521 26040 X – ISBN 0 521 27816 3 (pbk.)
1. Aeneas (Legendary character) – Poetry.   1. Gransden, K. W.
II. Title.   III. Series.
PA6803.B31G73   1991
883′.01–DC20   90-23826
CIP

ISBN 0 521 26040 X hardback
ISBN 0 521 27816 3 paperback

A O

# CONTENTS

# PREFACE

This edition has been long in the making. After starting it, in 1978, I realised how much more I needed to understand about the still relatively neglected second half of the *Aeneid*. I therefore set my work on book XI aside and wrote a book on the second half of the poem (*Virgil's Iliad*, Cambridge 1984). I then resumed this edition, but set it aside once more to contribute the volume on the *Aeneid* in the 'Landmarks of World Literature' series (Cambridge 1990). During these years there was a spate of new publications on Virgil, many of them coinciding with the bimillennium of the poet's death (variously computed at 1981 and 1982): I have tried to take account of as much of this material as I could manage. Thus revised and updated, this edition is now offered in the hope that it will enable more readers to respond to the splendours of the later Virgil.

Among many and various debts over the years, I must single out that to Professor Kenney, whose advice, patience and encouragement through successive stages of the Commentary have been invaluable to me. Dr Penelope Murray and the late R. D. Williams read an earlier draft of the Introduction and made many helpful suggestions. Dr N. Horsfall allowed me to see an early version of his paper on Camilla and gave me the benefit of his unrivalled knowledge of Virgil's antiquarian sources. The staff of Bodley's Library and of the Library of the Institute of Classical Studies, London, helped me to track down various elusive items, including the early volumes of the new *Enciclopedia Virgiliana*, which few British libraries will probably ever buy. Jenny Wagstaffe of the Oxford University Press kindly provided me with a copy of the most recent reprint of the Oxford Text of Virgil. I should also like to thank Susan Moore for the care and thoroughness with which she sub-edited the final typescript. She has saved me from many errors and inconsistencies.

In conclusion, I should state that I have tried, in the Introduction to this edition, to avoid repeating findings – especially concerning Virgil's poetic technique – already published in my edition of book VIII, in the present series. Some duplication has proved unavoidable; but the two Introductions may perhaps be regarded to some extent as complementary, though the second assumes no knowledge of the first.

*1991*

K.W.G.

# INTRODUCTION

## 1. VIRGIL'S 'ILIAD'[1]

Virgil chose as the central figure of his epic poem the *Aeneid* the Trojan hero Aineias from Homer's *Iliad*; he survived the fall of Troy, 'for it is destined that he should escape, that the race of Dardanus might not perish ... and thus shall the might of Aineias reign among the Trojans, and his children's children who shall be born hereafter' (*Iliad* 20.302–8).[2] From the hint contained in these remarkable lines, Greek and Roman historians developed a tradition that Aeneas, after escaping from Troy, conveyed his father, his son and his household gods[3] safely to Italy (Hesperia, the land of the west). There, three centuries or more before the legendary founding of Rome by Romulus, he established a settlement in Latium,[4] after defeating local opposition led by Turnus of Ardea, prince of the Rutuli.

V.'s genius led him to see in this story the possibility of combining into a single work Homer's two epics, but in reverse order: first Aeneas' wanderings westward from Troy to Latium, his 'Odyssey', then his war with the Latins, his 'Iliad'. The story also provided the poet with ample opportunity to develop Aeneas' two chief characteristics, his prowess at arms and his *pietas*.[5] The *Aeneid* quickly established itself as Rome's national epic.

In the poem's grand design, then, the second half, which the poet signals self-consciously with the words

> dicam horrida bella,
> dicam acies actosque animis in funera reges ...

---

[1] For a fuller treatment of what must here be briefly summarised see Otis 318–82; Gransden, *VI passim*.

[2] 'Aeneas was unique among the Trojans in that he had a future as well as a past' (Grant 68–9).

[3] On the *penates* see, e.g., Galinsky 147–8, Alföldi 258.

[4] On the cult of Aeneas in Lavinium see Alföldi 256–65.

[5] On Aeneas' *pietas*, first mentioned by Homer, *Il.* 20.297–9, see N. Horsfall, 'Some problems in the Aeneas legend', *C.Q.* n.s. 29 (1979) 372–90; Galinsky 3–61.

> ... maior rerum mihi nascitur ordo,
> maius opus moueo.                    $(7.41-5)^6$

is the 'Italian' half of the poem, the poem of war, in which Aeneas, albeit reluctant to fight another war, inaugurates the historic world-mission of Rome as foretold him by his father Anchises in the underworld:

> tu regere imperio populos, Romane, memento
> (hae tibi erunt artes), pacique imponere morem,
> parcere subiectis et debellare superbos.[7]
>
> $(6.851-3)$

The 'greater sequence of events', the 'greater work', which Virgil proclaimed near the beginning of the second half of his poem, is, then, a Roman 're-enactment' of Homer's *Iliad*,[8] as prophesied to Aeneas by the Sibyl at the start of his visit to the underworld:

> bella, horrida bella,
> et Thybrim multo spumantem sanguine cerno.
> non Simois tibi nec Xanthus nec Dorica castra
> defuerint; alius Latio iam partus Achilles ...
>
> $(6.86-9)$

The repeated cycle of events recalls the Sibylline prophecy in the poet's earlier fourth Eclogue of the forthcoming 'second heroic age':

> erunt etiam altera bella,
> atque iterum ad Troiam magnus mittetur Achilles.
>
> (*Ecl.* 4.35-6)

But the 'second Achilles already born in Latium' referred to in the Sibyl's prophecy in *Aeneid* VI is Turnus; and in this second Iliad Achilles will be defeated and the Trojan hero, Hector's successor, will be victo-

---

[6] V. may here have been expressing 'a Callimachean scruple against undertaking a work of Iliadic magnitude' (Clausen 14).

[7] On these famous lines see N. Rudd, 'The idea of empire in the *Aeneid*', in *Virgil in a cultural tradition*, edd. R. A. Cardwell and J. Hamilton (Nottingham 1986) 28–42; R. D. Williams, *The Aeneid* (London 1987) 39–40.

[8] That the *Aeneid* was to be 'greater than the *Iliad*' was proclaimed by Propertius, 2.34.66 *nescio quid maius nascitur Iliade*. For Virgil's allusions to Homer see G. Knauer's summary of his *Die Aeneis und Homer*, 'Virgil's *Aeneid* and Homer', *G.R.B.S.* 5 (1964) 64–84.

rious, the fall of Troy will be avenged and the way opened for a second Troy to arise one day beside the Tiber, the Rome of Caesar Augustus.

The *Iliad* is the story of 'the wrath of Achilles', announced by Homer as his theme in the opening invocation. But the events generated by the 'wrath-theme' occupy only a part of the poem: they form a carefully structured sequence, embedded in a narrative of immense length containing may characters and episodes which are tangential to the main story, though appropriate in a poem which is, after all, entitled the *Iliad* and *not* the 'Achilleid'. The main story begins in book I, with a quarrel between Achilles and the Greek commander-in-chief Agamemnon over a woman, a prize of war – a quarrel which itself reflects the larger quarrel between Greeks and Trojans over Helen, the cause of the Trojan war. Forced to surrender his prize, Achilles, angry at loss of face, withdraws from the fighting, though remaining in Troy; his mother Thetis exacts from Zeus a promise to give temporary aid to the Trojans; they consequently enjoy a run of victories under Hector, their greatest hero – a cruelly delusive twist, for Hector after a spectacular but brief hour of glory (*aristeia*) in which he kills Achilles' closest comrade Patroclus, is himself killed by Achilles, who returns to the fight to avenge his friend. The fall of Hector foreshadows the fall of Troy itself, though this lies outside the scope of Homer's epic, which ends with a truce: Achilles returns Hector's body to king Priam, and both sides dispose of their dead.[9]

Virgil used the story of Achilles, Hector and Patroclus in his version of Aeneas' war in Latium. He eliminated Homer's wrath-theme though not, of course, wrath in its larger sense: indeed war-madness, *furor*, the hero raging on the battlefield, is the most powerful motif of the closing books of the *Aeneid*. But his hero Aeneas, the man of *pietas*, could not be portrayed as quarrelling, sulking or withdrawing from the fight out of pique: such behaviour might befit a Homeric hero, but not an ur-Roman. Aeneas is indeed absent from the battlefield when the war starts, in book IX; but he is absent on a proper Roman-style diplomatic mission, seeking allies in a war not of his choosing. When he arrived in Italy (book VII) Latinus king of the Latins recognised him as the foreign prince (*dux externus*) destined by fate and foretold by the oracles to be the husband of his daughter Lavinia and co-ruler with him and future

[9] For a fuller account see Silk 32–46.

master of Italy. Latinus welcomed Aeneas, rejecting the claims of an earlier suitor, Turnus, who had the support of the queen, Amata. Since Aeneas' ancestor Dardanus was supposed by Virgil to have emigrated originally from Italy to Troy, Aeneas' arrival there could be seen as a *nostos* or homecoming;[10] Lavinia thus assumes a kind of subsidiary role as a second Penelope, with the rival suitors of Homer's *Odyssey* reduced to one, Turnus. But Lavinia is more significantly to be seen as a second Helen, the 'cause of so much evil' referred to by the Sibyl in her prophecy:

> causa mali tanti coniunx iterum hospita Teucris
> externique iterum thalami.          (6.93–4)

Turnus, prompted by a Fury sent by Juno (the Roman equivalent of Homer's implacably anti-Trojan Hera), rouses the local tribes to arms against the newcomers,[11] despite Latinus' protests, and *Aeneid* VII ends with a 'catalogue' or parade of the Italian leaders, led by Mezentius and with Turnus and Camilla bringing up the rear. The whole 'catalogue' is thus framed by Aeneas' three principal opponents: Mezentius dies in book X, Camilla in book XI and Turnus at the end of book XII.

Meanwhile Aeneas makes alliances: first with the Arcadian settler Evander, whose little kingdom on the site of the future Rome he visits in book VIII. Evander entrusts his son Pallas to Aeneas' protection. Aeneas then goes to Etruria and forms an alliance with king Tarchon, with whom he returns to the battlefield in book X. During the fierce fighting which now ensues, Turnus kills Pallas. Aeneas' debt of honour to Evander thus gives him further motivation (in addition to dynastic necessity) for killing Turnus at the end of the poem.

The war in Latium occupies the last four books of the *Aeneid*. It lasts only a few days, and here Virgil shows his mastery of narrative technique. In the annalistic tradition this war consisted of several campaigns spread over a number of years. Virgil has dramatically compressed and concentrated these diffuse stories into a highly structured sequence,

---

[10] Cf. Knauer 142–4, 239; H. Boas, *Aeneas' arrival in Latium* (Amsterdam 1938) 79–90. No source has yet been found for V.'s theory that the Trojans originated in Italy: see N. Horsfall, 'Corythus: the return of Aeneas in Virgil and his sources', *J.R.S.* 63 (1973) 74–9.

[11] On the actual *casus belli*, the shooting by Ascanius of a pet stag belonging to the daughter of king Latinus' chief herdsman, see N. Horsfall, 'Virgil and the conquest of chaos', *Antichthon* 15 (1981) 149–50.

modifying the order of events and the roles of the chief characters in order to produce a kind of re-enactment of the *Iliad*. Thus in the *Aeneid* the killing of Mezentius by Aeneas is only a prelude to the final climactic killing of Turnus,[12] whereas in earlier versions he was the leader of the Etruscans and was finally killed by Ascanius.[13] But Virgil wanted the Etruscans to be Aeneas' allies,[14] so he made Tarchon their chief (perhaps because of his legendary links with the poet's home town of Mantua) and Mezentius a dispossessed tyrant who took refuge with Turnus. The role and character of Latinus were also considerably modified (see below, 16–17); as for Pallas, although his name had long been associated with the name of Pallanteum, his father's settlement on the Palatine (see *Aeneid* VIII), his 'Iliadic' significance as the Patroclus-figure in Aeneas' war is Virgil's invention, his death at the hand of Turnus, subsequently avenged by Aeneas, being modelled on the killing of Patroclus by Hector, subsequently avenged by Achilles.[15] Pallas' death in *Aeneid* x provides an example (cf. also the deaths of Nisus and Euryalus in book IX and Lausus in book x) of the poem's strongest anti-war motif, the pathos of those who die young: a motif which first appears in book VI in Anchises' reference to the untimely death of Marcellus, Augustus' heir-designate (6.968–86).

## 2. THE CLOSING BOOKS

The qualities we admire in the *Aeneid* do not, however, depend solely upon an awareness, important though this is, of the poem's 'intertextuality', of the way it transforms its Homeric models; nor upon a

[12] Mezentius' place at the head of the 'catalogue' in book VII testifies to his traditional pre-eminence in Aeneas' campaign: cf. Heinze 179; Alföldi 209–10; Grant 73–4.

[13] According to Servius (on 9. 742) the facts as given by Cato in his *Origines* were that Turnus was killed first, then Latinus, then Mezentius: cf. Ogilvie 34; *EV* I 708–11 s.v. 'Catone'; Heinze 172.

[14] On V.'s pro-Etruscan sympathies see Grant 72–6.

[15] According to Dion. Hal. 1.32–3, 39 Pallas was Evander's grandson, eponymous founder of the Palatine, where he was supposed to have been buried; his father was Hercules, his mother Evander's daughter Lavinia (*sic*). Latinus was also said to have been a grandson of Evander. There was evidently considerable conflation (and confusion) of the early Roman foundation-legends with the Arcadian founding of Rome as Pallanteum, narrated by V.'s Evander in *Aen.* VIII. See further Grant 44–6; Heinze 178–9; Knauer 249–52, 298–301.

complete grasp of the complex antiquarian sources on which the poet drew for the Italian second half of his epic. Transcending these, and especially conspicuous in the closing books, is the reader's growing awareness of the pervasive and empathising presence in the text of the 'implied author'.[16] This figure is not to be identified with the narrator who organises the sequence of events, who tells us that dawn came or that a man died; nor the self-conscious composer of epic (*dicam . . . horrida bella*); nor the speculative philosopher who bequeathed to Dante the first full-scale realisation in poetry of the soul's odyssey after death; but rather the omnipresent sensibility of a creative artist continually involved in every possible nuance of his own text, continually evolving new modes of insight into the human condition: the poet (for example) of the flower-simile in book XI (see Comm. on 68–71) which Page thought 'perhaps the most perfect simile in the poem'; the poet who could transform a traditional *topos* into a sentiment in which the reader may find his own experience expressed:

> Aurora interea miseris mortalibus almam
> extulerat lucem referens opera atque labores.
> (11.182–3)

the poet who could write of 'war and the pity of war':

> di Iouis in tectis iram miserantur inanem
> amborum et tantos mortalibus esse labores.
> (10.758–9)

Moreover, Virgil brought to the composition of his 'Homeric' epic an apprenticeship in 'Alexandrian' miniaturism (his eclogues or pastorals) and a sensibility cultivated by a study of the poetry and principles of Callimachus (who reacted against poems of Homeric length) and of his Latin imitators, the so-called 'neoteroi', of whom Catullus is the greatest survivor. The features of this poetry include stylistic polish and elegance, attention to detail, and a subjectivity of treatment which might fairly be called romantic. Such techniques are conspicuous in the *Aeneid*, and indeed Clausen has suggested that Virgil produced 'an extension of Callimachean poetics into an area (full-length epic) precluded by Callimachus'.[17] This remarkable fusion of opposites, Homer

---

[16] Cf. Gransden, *VI* 155–6.     [17] Clausen 14.

and Callimachus, produced a poem 'vibrant with tension between ...
Augustan sense and Alexandrian sensibility, between faith and irony'.[18]

In the last three books of the *Aeneid* Virgil's art is at its most intense
and fully developed. If books VI and VIII are the most Roman books of
the poem, books X, XI, and XII are the most Italian. The centrepiece of
this 'triptych', book XI, is the most varied in tone and content, a splendid
intermezzo between the unrelievedly sombre and war-dominated tenth
and twelfth books.[19] The opening sequence, Aeneas' triumph over the
body of Mezentius, and Pallas' funeral, completes the events of book
X but needed to be separated from them by a new start and a new day
so as not to spoil the climax of book X, the death of Mezentius. At
the Latin war-council which completes the first half of book XI, it is
proposed that Turnus should agree to a truce and engage in single
combat with Aeneas to decide the fate of Lavinia and the control of
Latium (an Iliadic theme based on the truce in *Iliad* III and the abortive
duel between Paris and Menelaus to decide the fate of Helen). Turnus
accepts this proposal, but not until the beginning of book XII; meanwhile, hostilities are resumed and occupy the rest of book XI. Turnus
plans a double manoeuvre: he will ambush Aeneas while Camilla leads
a cavalry attack. But the manoeuvre fails; Camilla, after a brilliant but
short-lived *aristeia*, is killed, the Rutuli are routed and Turnus has to
abandon the ambush. A direct confrontation between Aeneas and
Turnus is postponed by nightfall, which ends the book. This, the poem's
final encounter, was foreseen and promised in book X, but the destined
hour has not yet arrived, as it has still not arrived in book XI. In book
X Jupiter reminds Hercules, to whom Pallas has prayed in vain for help,
that

> stat sua cuique dies, breue et inreparabile tempus
> omnibus est uitae ...
>
>                     ... etiam sua Turnum
> fata uocant metasque dati peruenit ad aeui.
>
>                   (10.467–72)

The past tense, *peruenit*, implies that, although he does not yet know it,
Turnus has already reached his appointed 'date with destiny'. The

[18] Newman, *CET* 187.

[19] Heinze 227; Pöschl 102; Guillemin 301 '... toute est vie, mouvement,
lignes, couleurs ... une surface large, unie, lumineuse'.

reader can imagine him already there. In Jupiter's words, a moving articulation of the human condition, we hear again, unmistakably, the voice of the implied author. And when Turnus has killed Pallas, the poet himself speaks to the reader:

> nescia mens hominum fati sortisque futurae ...
> Turno tempus erit magno cum optauerit emptum
> intactum Pallanta ...                    (10.501–4).

The author here comments proleptically on the inevitable end of his own narrative. The time that will come for Turnus is time as *kairos* as well as time as *chronos*: Turnus' 'time' is not just calendar time but significant time; it is the narrator's arrival at the planned, promised and (temporarily) postponed climax of his story.[20]

There is comparatively little divine intervention in the closing books of the *Aeneid*. In book XI the gods hardly appear. Only the scene between the nymph Opis and the goddess Diana takes place *sedibus in superis*. Indeed, the killing by Opis of Camilla's slayer is the only example in the poem of a hero's death being brought about directly by a divine being.[21]

But Diana could not prevent Camilla's death. In the council of the gods which opens the last three books of the poem (10.1–117), Jupiter announced that he would remain impartial in the war between Trojans and Latins, a war he had not willed and had indeed forbidden: *quae contra uetitum discordia?* he asked, as Venus and Juno angrily argued their cases. Jupiter's decree was that, the war having started, it must be played out to its end by the heroes themselves, and that he would make no distinction between the two sides, who at the end of book XII are destined to become a single nation, first Italian, then Roman.

> quae cuique est fortuna hodie, quam quisque secat spem,
> Tros Rutulusne fuat, nullo discrimine habebo ...
>                    ... sua cuique exorsa laborem
> fortunamque ferent. rex Iuppiter omnibus idem.
> fata uiam inuenient.                    (10.107–13)

---

[20] Cf. F. Kermode, *The sense of an ending* (Oxford 1967) 46–50; Gransden, *VI* 195.

[21] See also Comm. on 836–7. At 725–8 Jupiter arouses Tarchon: a 'divine prompting' to heroic action (see Comm.).

'Then, whatever each man's fortune is today, the hope each pursues, Trojan or Rutulian, let him carve it out, I'll make no distinction ... Whatever each sets his hand to will bring him toil and fortune. King Jupiter is the same for all men. Fate will find the way.' With these momentous words Jupiter removes himself from the conflict and sets the heroes free to enact history.[22] The last three books of the poem are the working out of this programme. Although in book x Juno is allowed to perform an 'Iliadic' rescue of Turnus from the field, she is specifically warned by Jupiter not to assume from this temporary respite that Turnus' fate is rescinded (she does hope this, for unlike Jupiter she has no insight into the future but remains fixated on the past). When Pallas faced Turnus he died because he met a more experienced soldier; when Lausus faced Aeneas he attempted *maiora ... uiribus* (more than he had strength for, 10.811).

## 3. BOOK XI[23]

### (i) Structure

The action of the book occupies four days, of which two are merely summarised. Day 1 (vv. 1–181) describes Pallas' funeral, days 2 and 3 (vv. 182–209) the truce and burial of the dead. Day 4 comprises the remainder of the book (vv. 210–915): the Latin war-council, the resumption of hostilities, Turnus' plan to ambush Aeneas, the *aristeia* and death of Camilla. The book thus offers one of the most clearly defined triadic structures in the poem:

1. Funeral and truce (1–224)
    (i) Aeneas' triumph over Mezentius (1–28)
    (ii) The funeral of Pallas (29–181)
    (iii) The burial of the dead (182–224)
2. The council of war (225–531)
    (i) Report of the embassy (225–301)

---

[22] Cf. Gransden, *VI* 130–8; C. H. Wilson, 'Jupiter and the fates', *C. Q.* N.S. 29 (1979) 361–71.

[23] A useful summary is in M. di Cesare, *The altar and the city* (1974) 198–210, though he overstresses the book's inconclusiveness. Heinze sums up fairly (453): the separate sections are sharply distinguished but the narrative is continuous.

Various formal and thematic parallels may be seen between the first and second halves of the poem, whereby, for example, book XI, penultimate book of the 'Iliadic' second half, offers correspondences with book v, penultimate book of the 'Odyssean' first half.[24] Both are interludes: book v separates Aeneas' two most significant 'Odyssean' experiences, his encounter with Dido and his visit to the underworld, while book XI separates his two greatest 'Iliadic' feats of prowess, against Mezentius and Turnus. *Aeneid* v also included funeral games (in honour of Anchises): Homer's funeral games occur not in the *Odyssey* but in the penultimate book of the *Iliad* (in honour of Patroclus) and it might have been expected that Virgil would follow this example and include funeral games for Pallas in book XI: but the relaxed tone of heroic games, entirely appropriate to Homeric narrative and Homeric decorum in *Iliad* 23, would have been out of place in the powerful and dramatic sequence of events which form book XI; nor would the narrative have accommodated the digression.[25]

Structural parallels within the last three books of the poem are also evident. Each ends with the death of one of the principal leaders of the Italian alliance: Mezentius, Camilla, Turnus. Moreover, the deaths of Camilla in book XI and Turnus in book XII are given the same line as epitaph: *uitaque cum gemitu fugit indignata sub umbras* (11.831 = 12.952).[26] As this is also the last line of the poem, its occurrence in the death of Camilla works for the reader somewhat like a symphonic 'false ending'.

[24]  On structural parallels see Gransden, *Aen. VIII* 6–7; Camps 37–60.

[25]  Virgil's funeral games in *Aen.* v include the so-called *lusus Troiae*, an equestrian display which offers a 'mock prefiguration' of the cavalry action in book XI. On the original connection between the 'Trojan games' and the cavalry, see Alföldi 281–2.

[26]  Virgil here clearly echoes Homer, who gave Patroclus and Hector the same three-line 'epitaph': *Il.* 16.855–7 = *Il.* 22.361–3.

### (ii) The funeral of Pallas

The funeral of Pallas corresponds structurally and thematically with the funeral of Patroclus in the *Iliad* (with some undertones also of the funeral of Hector). Pallas' death touches Aeneas deeply, but this was no boyhood friendship like that of Achilles and Patroclus. They met for the first time at Pallanteum in book VIII. Patroclus was in fact older than Achilles, though a lesser warrior;[27] Pallas was a young untried hero, entrusted to Aeneas' protection by his father Evander:

> hunc tibi praeterea, spes et solacia nostri,
> Pallanta adiungam; sub te tolerare magistro
> militiam et graue Martis opus, tua cernere facta
> adsuescat, primis et te miretur ab annis.

> (8.514–17)

Evander's words carry a note of sad irony in the light of future events (in book X): Aeneas had no time to teach or to protect his protégé; Turnus got to him first. But Aeneas was not refusing to fight, or absent from the field, when Pallas was killed; nor did Pallas fight in Aeneas' armour or in any sense play a role, as Patroclus in *Iliad* XVI had 'played' Achilles in his friend's armour. For the implied author of the *Aeneid*, Pallas' death is primarily an example of war's tragic futility, like the deaths of Nisus and Euryalus in book IX. It is the tragedy of those who die untried, and it brings Virgil closer in spirit to Wilfred Owen than to Homer:

> Your slender attitude
>   Trembles not exquisite like limbs knife-skewed,
> Rolling and rolling there ...
> Till the fierce love they bear
>   Cramps them in death's extreme decrepitude.[28]

In Homer extreme youth is not so much stressed; the heroes of the *Iliad* have, after all, been fighting for nearly ten years, while some were already the veterans of earlier campaigns.

[27] See *Il.* 11.786.
[28] For another 'Virgilian' passage from Owen, see Gransden, *VA* 61.

Nowhere in the entire *Aeneid* is the voice of the implied author more powerfully present than in the opening section of book XI, an immense symphonic adagio.[29] The reader accompanies the funeral procession on its winding course back to Pallanteum and the grief of the waiting Evander, whose fearful premonition that he might outlive his son (8.572–83) is now a reality. It is hard to see how pathos could be taken further than this; and it is sustained throughout the scene on the battlefield and the truce for the burial of the dead, where the lurid and flickering light of many fires picks out the desolate landscape. This truce is a Homeric feature: in *Iliad* III there is a truce before the duel between Paris and Menelaus, and in *Iliad* XXIV there is a twelve-day truce so that the Trojans may bury and mourn Hector. There is also a general truce for the burning of the dead in *Iliad* VII, after the duel between Hector and Ajax; this truce is granted to Priam by Agamemnon, as the truce in *Aeneid* XI is granted to Latinus by Aeneas, in both cases through a messenger: in *Iliad* VII the herald Idaios, in *Aeneid* XI unnamed *oratores*. Idaios makes it clear that after the truce the war will continue since Paris will not give up Helen; nor can Aeneas relinquish his claim to Lavinia and the leadership of Italy. Paris' claim to Helen is neither lawful nor underwritten by fate, and this is one of Virgil's most significant transformations of Homer.

The first part of book XI is dominated by Aeneas, who then disappears from the narrative (at 224), to reappear briefly at the end (896–915). For the rest of the book the scene changes first to the headquarters of the Latin forces and then to the cavalry engagement. The Aeneas who presides over the funeral rites has seemed to some critics a very different figure from the man of blood and violence who at the end of book X killed Lausus and Mezentius. But we should not assume that Aeneas the warrior represents a temporary aberration from Aeneas the man of *pietas*. Virgil's intention was to give equal weight to the two traditional aspects of the character of this epic hero, described by the Sibyl (6.403) as *Troius Aeneas pietate insignis et armis* and addressed by Drances (11.125) in similar vein: '*iustitiaene prius mirer belline laborum?*' Aeneas behaves appropriately to the occasion; with dignity, sorrow and magnanimity during periods of peace, with ferocity on the battlefield. Virgil could not have presented, as the first founder of the Roman people, a hero

[29] See further Gransden, *VI* 154–73.

whose heart was not wholly in whatever fate required of him, in war or peace. The Virgilian *Iliad* would have been unthinkable without the *aristeia* of the principal hero; and although in book XI Aeneas has sad business to transact and no fighting to do, his first speech (14–28) is an exhortation to his men to further deeds of prowess couched in tones confident to the point of self-vaunting: '*manibusque meis Mezentius hic est*'; so far is he from forgetting or regretting his conduct at the end of book X.

## (iii) The council of war

This, the most important debate in the poem, is a conflation of three Homeric war-councils.[30] In *Iliad* VII Antenor proposes the return of Helen, but Paris refuses, and this message is duly conveyed to the Greeks. That council also occurs during a truce, but it is not crucial to the narrative at that point in the poem, whereas the council in *Aen.* XI is crucial,[31] for it leads – after the interlude of the cavalry engagement – directly into the truce at the opening of book XII, in which Aeneas and Turnus prepare for their final confrontation. (This truce the Rutuli sacrilegiously break.)

In the war-council in *Iliad* XVII, as in *Aen.* XI, two opposing views on the war are put forward; the more prudent, the 'Antenorian' one, comes this time from Polydamas, but he is overruled by Hector. In the debate in *Aen.* XI the role of Hector is taken by Turnus, who overrules the sensible, albeit ill-motivated, advice of Drances, that the Latins should seek peace with the Trojans, leaving Turnus to face Aeneas in single combat (which does, of course, finally come about in book XII). The Homeric parallel is, however, further complicated by the fact that Drances' taunts against Turnus sometimes recall Hector's taunts against Paris (in *Iliad* III) for his reluctance to face Menelaus in single combat.

There remains the curious council in *Iliad* II in which Agamemnon tests his troops by suggesting that they should withdraw from the war.[32]

[30] For a detailed commentary on the Homeric parallels see P. Schenk, *Die Gestalt Turnus in Vergils Aeneis* (Königstein 1984) 119–146.

[31] Cf. Gransden, *VI* 174–9.

[32] On the problems raised by this passage see M. M. Willcock, *A companion to the Iliad* (Chicago and London 1976) 17–18; G. S. Kirk, *Homer and the epic* (Cambridge 1965) 160–1.

Agamemnon is there abused by Thersites, described as 'the ugliest man who came to Ilion', but a fluent orator, albeit one who spoke chiefly for effect. He abuses Agamemnon, echoing Achilles' attack on him in the quarrel scene in book 1. Some elements of Thersites' role and even of his character may be seen in Drances,[33] though the latter is a much more powerful orator.

Drances occurs only here.[34] He is presented as a clever speaker and a man of influence: as a member of the council, he is closer to Homer's Polydamas than to his Thersites (Polydamas is described as 'a better speaker than Hector', *Il.* 18.252). Virgil describes him in some detail:[35] his portrait offers a hostile presentation of the *nouus homo*, a class well known in the late republic. The term was ambiguous, but in its more general and usual sense meant someone who had achieved senatorial rank without any senatorial antecedents. Such men often came from obscurity, but sometimes married into the *nobilitas* as Drances' father, himself unknown, is said to have done.[36]

In the 'Invective against Sallust' attributed to Cicero, the author claims that, even if his ancestors were previously unknown, 'I would give them fame' (*si prius noti non fuerunt, a me accipiant initium memoriae suae*).[37] In a note on Drances, Heyne records that Julius Sabinus identified his mother as king Latinus' sister and his father as a countryman 'nescio unde'. The *nouus* had to excel either as a soldier or as a lawyer or as an orator; he also needed money to fulfil his ambitions (Drances is *largus opum*, 11.338). It was suggested in the Renaissance that Drances was intended by Virgil as a portrait of Cicero, with Turnus as Antony; this is very doubtful; but what is certain is that in his portrait of Drances, and in his exchange with Turnus, Virgil drew on the

---

[33] Achilles' hatred of Thersites is reflected in Turnus' hatred of Drances: cf. *Il.* 2.220, *Aen.* 11.336–7. But the parallel should not be pushed too far: cf. Highet 248–51.

[34] On Drances see further A. La Penna, *EV* II 138–40 s.v. 'Drance'; A. La Penna, 'Spunti sociologici per l'interpretazione dell'Eneide', in *Vergiliana*, ed. H. Bardon and R. Verdière (Leiden 1971) 283–8; Paratore on 11.336.

[35] 'The analysis of Drances' character and motives is wholly exceptional': Quinn 309, 240–2.

[36] Cf. T. P. Wiseman, *New men in the Roman senate* (Oxford 1971) 53 'the wives and mothers of *noui* were seldom referred to except for their nobility or notoriety'.

[37] *Inuectiua in Sallustium* 2.5, printed in *Appendix Sallustiana* ed. A. Kurfess (Teubner, Leipzig 1962).

language of demagogy and polemic. The 'Invective against Cicero' attributed to Sallust contains an interesting passage on Cicero, the *homo nouus Arpinas*:

> ... homo leuissimus, supplex inimicis, amicis contumeliosus, modo harum, modo illarum partium, fidus nemini, leuissimus senator, mercennarius patronus ... lingua uana, manus rapacissimae ... pedes fugaces.[38]

Similar words are used by Turnus against Drances:

> an tibi Mauors
> uentosa in lingua pedibusque fugacibus istis
> semper erit?                            (11.389–91)

Virgil's treatment of Drances is, however, characteristically ambiguous, for he espouses, albeit primarily out of hatred for Turnus, the cause of peace, using what sounds like heartfelt language: *nulla salus bello, pacem te poscimus omnes*. His ambivalence was imitated by Milton in the portrait of Belial, who appears in the role of peacemaker in the debate in Pandemonium in *Paradise Lost* II, itself modelled on the council in *Aeneid* XI.

Apart from Drances and Turnus, the other speakers in the council are king Latinus and the envoy Venulus, who begins the debate by reporting on his mission to the Greek veteran Diomedes, now settled at Arpi, with whom the Italians had sought an alliance. (This is the return of the embassy despatched at the beginning of book VIII.) Venulus gives Diomedes' own words – a powerful anti-war speech of central importance to the closing books of the *Aeneid*. Anti-war sentiments, after all, come far more effectively from a victorious than from a defeated leader. Diomedes reflects on the bitter aftermath of the Trojan war, the disasters and tribulations which befell the returning Greeks, culminating in the murder of Agamemnon by his wife Clytaemnestra and her lover Aegisthus (a motif which runs through Homer's *Odyssey*). Telemachus' missions to Nestor and Menelaus in *Odyssey* III and IV provided Virgil with models for reminiscences by Greek survivors of misfortunes suffered by themselves and their comrades after the fall of Troy: the

---

[38] *Inuectiua in Ciceronem* 3.5, printed in *Appendix Sallustiana* (see n. 37), ascribed to Sallust in the MSS and cited as genuine by Quintilian.

incidents referred to by Diomedes were treated in post-Iliadic epics now lost and by the tragedians.

Diomedes pays tribute to Aeneas' military prowess, and reminds the Latins that it was Hector and Aeneas who were mainly responsible for the fact that it took the Greeks ten years to beat the Trojans. The mutual respect of Diomedes and Aeneas is an important motif in the *Aeneid*: in his first speech in book I, Aeneas apostrophises Diomedes as *Danaum fortissime gentis* (1.95) and wishes he had died at his hands in Troy (as indeed he nearly did, see *Il.* 5.297), and at 2.197 ranks him with Achilles. Diomedes emphasises not only Aeneas' personal prowess but also the rightness of the Trojan cause. There is no mention of the theft of the Palladium (referred to in the *Aeneid* by the discredited Sinon, 2.163–70), and there was a tradition that Diomedes, realising that his possession of the holy relic was accursed, returned it to Aeneas through Nautes.[39]

Diomedes does, however, mention his wounding of Aeneas' mother Aphrodite (*Iliad* 5.330–51). In his regret for this act of impiety and his heartfelt plea for peace he is the type of the 'reformed' Greek hero (as the Ulysses of *Aeneid* II is the type of the 'unregenerate' one). After the war-council breaks up, the women of Italy, led by queen Amata, pray to the goddess Athene to 'break the spear of the Trojan pirate' (Aeneas), exactly as the Trojan women had prayed to the same goddess to break the spear of Diomedes (*Iliad* 6.297–310), who during the absence of Achilles was the most feared of the Greek heroes. This allusion allows the role of the Homeric Diomedes (whom Virgil has now written out of his own *Iliad*) to devolve upon Aeneas. Moreover, the Homeric scene of supplication has already figured in the *Aeneid*: it is one of the scenes from the Trojan war represented in Juno's temple at Carthage which Aeneas had contemplated in troubled wonder together with representations of Diomedes, Achilles and the Amazon Penthesilea (1.479–82).

Virgil's Latinus is very different from the Latinus of earlier tradition. According to Cato he offered the Trojans a piece of land, which they accepted; but they trespassed beyond this, so Latinus was forced into a war and was killed. The offer of land is retained by Virgil: it is mentioned at 7.262 and again in the king's peace-proposals in book XI (316–23) in which he also praises the Italian war-effort. This speech

---

[39] See Austin's n. on 2.163.

preserves traces of a more vigorous Latinus found in earlier Roman writers, though it also works as a diplomatic face-saving gesture towards Turnus.[40]

Virgil could not easily have retained, in his story of *pius* Aeneas, the story that Aeneas fought against, or caused the death of, his future father-in-law. In *Aeneid* VII Latinus is introduced as an old man, the Italian counterpart of king Priam, and, in his love of peace, resembling the Arcadian king Evander, Pallas' father. His pacifism is an important element in Virgil's account, for it helps to emphasise and isolate the *uiolentia* of Turnus. Latinus gladly accepted the Trojans as allies on their first arrival in Latium; in permitting Turnus to go to war he acted against his better judgement, as he reiterates at the beginning of book XII: his words there, *arma impia sumpsi*, recall the combatant king of the earlier versions, but *impia* also operates in strong antithesis to Virgil's *pius* Aeneas, who thus retains the moral advantage throughout. Latinus is racked with guilt and despair; after the war-council in book XI he 'blamed himself for not firmly standing by his new son-in-law', and the reader will recall the irresistible war-lust visited on Turnus and the Italians in book VII by Juno through the Fury Allecto, against which Latinus was helpless: *frangimur heu fatis*, he lamented (7.594), and put the blame on his people.

The Latin war-council breaks up with the news that the Trojans are on the move again. Further discussion is now useless. Just as the assembly in *Iliad* II broke up with a speech from Nestor recommending a return to battle ('we fight with words only', a recurrent motif of the *Iliad* taken over by Virgil), so Turnus sneers at his fellow-chiefs for praising peace while the enemy advance.

The character of Turnus is that of a man wholly dedicated to self-interest. He pursues Aeneas as a sexual rival. He is shown as attractive to women: he is first introduced to the reader at 7.55 as *pulcherrimus* (an adjective he shares with Dido); he has charmed Latinus' queen Amata and is relaxed with Camilla, as appears from the easy tone of his briefing (11.508–19). The distinction between his type of courage and Aeneas' was a familiar moral *topos* in antiquity: thus Cicero (*De officiis* 1.62–3) criticises the man who fights for his own advantage, not the safety of all

---

[40] See further Servius on 11.316; Heinze 171–9; Grant 91–2; N. Horsfall, 'Virgil's conquest of chaos', *Antichthon* 15 (1981) 147.

(*pugnat ... non pro salute communi, sed pro suis commodis*), and quotes with approval Plato's distinction between true courage and rashness (*Laches* 197b): ... *animus paratus ad periculum, si sua cupiditate, non utilitate communi impellitur, audaciae potius nomen habeat quam fortitudinis*.[41]

Turnus is beyond doubt '*animus paratus ad periculum*'. In book XI he still thinks the risks are justified. He still thinks there are battles to be fought and won before he need accept Drances' view, that he must offer himself in single combat with Aeneas for the safety of all and the common good: a solution he finally accepts in book XII, after Camilla's death; even then he still blusters, blaming the Trojans for the delay in signing a treaty. But in book XI he still hopes for military success, he continues to stall, to play for time,[42] to throw in more troops (Camilla and her Volscian cavalry), keeping single combat in reserve as a last resort.

Structurally and thematically, the Latin war-council may also be seen as in some respects parallel to the council of the gods which opened book X. Like Jupiter in book X, king Latinus wants peace but lets the war go on. The violently opposed speeches of Drances and Turnus correspond to the speeches of Venus and Juno; each pair of speakers employs the same rhetorical trick of quoting and capping the previous speaker. But of course Jupiter's great decree of impartiality is quite different from Latinus' indecisiveness.

## (iv) The cavalry engagement

The final third of book XI, the cavalry engagement and the *aristeia* of Camilla, occupies nearly half the book's total length, but the tempo is much faster than that of the funeral and war-council scenes. It is perhaps Virgil's finest military set-piece, giving the lie to the view, still sometimes expressed, that he cannot write battle-poetry: '... a vast fresco ... revealing a narrative talent not fully realised in the earlier books and conveying to the reader an aesthetic joy which derives from the poet's mastery of his material'.[43] It is written in the poet's grandest

---

[41] Cf. Schweitzer 37–9. For a more favourable view of Turnus see Pöschl 93–5.

[42] On Turnus' 'brinkmanship' see Schweitzer 39 '... riss er sein ganz Volk an den Rand des Abgrundes'. On the opening of book XII and for more on Turnus' psychology see also Johnson 50–9.

[43] Guillemin 301.

style, with full-scale similes (721–4, 751–6) and a characteristically hyperbolic presentation,[44] derived from the *Iliad*, of the individual hero as a kind of 'one-man' (or in this case one-woman) army.[45]

There are structural and thematic correspondences with the *Iliad*. Camilla's death is a re-enactment of some aspects of the deaths of Sarpedon and Patroclus in *Iliad* xvi and thus to some extent 'doubles' the death of Pallas in *Aeneid* x. Arruns' prayer to Apollo to allow him to kill Camilla and return safely corresponds to Achilles' prayer on behalf of Patroclus in *Iliad* xvi, while the divine removal of Camilla's body to her homeland for burial is modelled on the divine removal of Sarpedon's body in the *Iliad*. Arruns' prayer, like Achilles', is only half granted: Patroclus kills Sarpedon but is himself killed by Hector, while Arruns kills Camilla but is himself killed by Opis. Apollo blinds Patroclus in a mist, and it is Apollo who allows Camilla to die: she too goes blindly (*caeca*, 781) to her doom. When Arruns kills her he assumes the Homeric role of Euphorbus, the otherwise unknown soldier who gave Patroclus his first wound and was subsequently killed; Arruns like Euphorbus is overcome with fear at his own deed and seeks refuge in flight (*fugit ... exterritus*, 806).

However, the cavalry action itself has no Homeric parallel. There are no cavalry in the *Iliad*:[46] horses are used chiefly, if not solely, to pull chariots. It seems from two passages in the poem that Homer supposed chariots to have been used at one time as a genuine fighting force,[47] and in the mass-formation fighting in book xi the poet appears to envisage fighting from chariots.[48] But most of the monomachies in the poem take place after the heroes have dismounted.

Virgil's treatment of the war in Latium combines Homeric and Roman features, and this 'telescoping' of history and legend is typical

[44] On the greater frequency of hyperbole in the last four books of the *Aeneid* see Hardie 246 n. 24.

[45] See Hardie 285–7.

[46] Nor, presumably, in the other lost Greek primary epics, though it is possible that Penthesilea, in the continuation of the *Iliad*, fought on horseback: the Amazons were indeed the earliest cavalry: see Klingner 585–6.

[47] *Il.* 4.297–309, 11.736–40; G. S. Kirk, *Homer and the oral tradition* (Cambridge 1976) 61.

[48] See *Il.* 11.150–1. Willcock says that this passage is rhetorical and that no real chariot fighting occurs in the *Iliad*, but see also W. K. Pritchett, *The Greek state at war* iv (1985) 11–14, 32–3.

of his technique throughout the *Aeneid*.[49] In fact, little or nothing is known of the Roman army in pre-Etruscan times or of any Bronze Age warfare in Italy. The Etruscans possessed war-chariots, but it is not certain if they used them for actual fighting and if so, how. Indeed, their survival in Etruria was itself something of an anachronism: in post-Mycenaean Greece they were replaced by cavalry, and the Roman army before the time of king Servius Tullius (*c.* 578–584 B.C.) depended chiefly on cavalry.[50] But as the stirrup had not been invented in antiquity, fighting from horseback must always have been somewhat precarious. It is to Servius Tullius that a radical change in the Roman army is attributed, the subordination of cavalry to infantry, and the introduction to Rome of a Greek-style hoplite army equipped with the round shields used by the Etruscans. However, two centuries later, Camillus (on whom see below) did reform and enlarge the cavalry.[51]

The main cavalry units in Aeneas' army are in the ranks of his Etruscan allies under Tarchon (11.504, 517, 729), though the Arcadians also sent cavalry. Among the Italians, besides Camilla and her Volsci, Messapus also leads a cavalry unit.[52] The Etruscan renegade Mezentius fights on horseback but Aeneas, unmounted, kills him. Turnus uses a war-chariot, appropriately for so Homeric a hero (12.326).

## (v) Camilla

Camilla, like Drances, occurs only in the *Aeneid*. One might have expected to find traces of so striking a figure in the legends of pre-Roman Italy, but none have been discovered, so that she may be regarded as an invention of the poet's,[53] one of his most brilliant achievements,

[49] See N. Horsfall, *EV* I 151–4 s.v. 'anacronismi'.

[50] For further discussion see C. Saulnier, *L'Armée et la guerre dans le monde étrusco-romain* (Paris 1980) 66–70, 109–112.

[51] See further A. D. Snodgrass, *Arms and armour of the Greeks* (1967) 46, 84–6; L. Keppie, *The making of the Roman army* (1984) 17; Ogilvie 43–8, 152–3.

[52] 11.518–19. At 7.691 Messapus is described as *equum domitor, Neptunia proles*.

[53] Arguments for the pre-existence of a Volscian and Roman myth of Camilla are put forward by G. Arrigoni, *Camilla, Amazzone e sacerdotessa di Diana* (Milan 1982), the fullest treatment to date. A.'s hypothesis has been criticised by N. Horsfall in his review of her book, *C.R.* N.S. 34 (1984) 61–2, and more fully in a later article, 'Camilla: o i limiti dell' invenzione', *Athenaeum* N.S. 66 (1988) 31–51.

though in creating her he drew on Greek mythological figures. But she remains the apotheosis of Italian heroism, the incarnation of Italian *uirtus*,[54] as proudly described by Numanus:

> durum a stirpe genus natos ad flumina primum
> deferimus saeuoque gelu duramus et undis;
> uenatu inuigilant pueri siluasque fatigant,
> flectere ludus equos et spicula tendere cornu.
>
> (9.603–6)

Camilla's father gave her a 'river-baptism' when she was a baby (11.547–63), while her prowess as rider and huntress are among her most conspicuous characteristics. As a female version of the young doomed hero, she has affinities with Lausus, also a rider: both her father Metabus (whose connection with Camilla and the Volsci is also not attested outside the *Aeneid*) and Lausus' father Mezentius were exiled,[55] and indeed the story of Mezentius may have been the poet's model for Metabus. Camilla also resembles Nisus in that he too was a hunter and protégé of Diana (to whom he prays at 9.404–9). Camilla's virginity is also emphasised, and here she is the anti-type of Dido. In *Aeneid* i Venus, disguised as a virgin huntress and compared to a Thracian maid, Harpalyce (like Camilla, swift of foot and daughter of an exiled father),[56] narrates to Aeneas the story of Dido, another queen and huntress. Moreover, when Dido herself appears in the poem (1.496) she bears the *pharetra*, as also do the disguised Venus and Camilla herself, while just after his encounter with Venus and just before his meeting with Dido Aeneas has been looking at representations of the *bellatrix* Amazon queen Penthesilea in Juno's temple at Carthage.

Camilla's tough, pastoral early life, dedicated to hunting and virginity, under the protection of Diana, offers affinities with Greek myth, for instance the Arcadian nymph Callisto, described by Ovid (*Metamorphoses* 2.415) as 'a soldier of Diana'. The *arma Dianae* borne by Camilla in battle may be seen as a misuse or perversion of the weapons of the chase, in contrast to the arms given to Aeneas in book viii by Venus.

[54] See Schweitzer 53–6.

[55] Each was *pulsus ob inuidiam*, 11.539, 10.582.

[56] There is no evidence earlier than the *Aeneid* for this princess: Servius' note on 1.317 is clearly derived from Camilla. See also Austin on 1.317, where it is suggested that Harpalyce might have been treated by Callimachus. On the two opposite feminine types cf. Włosok 87 n. 58.

Moreover, in returning from her pastoral exile to lead her people in battle, Camilla removes herself from the protection (though not from the love) of Diana, whereas Aeneas never ceases to be under the protection of Venus. Her swiftness of foot, her free, joyful Arcadian associations, emphasised in the description of her at the end of book VII (her only other appearance in the poem) suggest a parallel with another Greek figure, Atalanta. And her *aristeia* exemplifies another Greek literary motif taken over by the Romans, the deeds of heroic women. Into this tradition must be fitted her metamorphosis from huntress to warrior and her self-styled role as 'Amazon' (11.648–9).

Homer mentions Amazons twice. Priam recalls the battle between the Phrygians and the Amazons at *Iliad* 3.189, while at 6.186 they are mentioned as having fought with Bellerophon; the same epithet, ἀντιάνειραι, 'who fight against men', occurs in both passages. Virgil describes Penthesilea at *Aen.* 1.493 in a phrase which seems to translate Homer's epithet, *audet . . . uiris concurrere uirgo.*

The most famous of the Amazons, Penthesilea, to whom Camilla is explicitly compared, does not figure in the *Iliad*, but her late entry into the Trojan war (Camilla's entry into the Latin war is also, comparatively speaking, 'late') is attested by the scholiast on *Iliad* 24.804 in the variant reading ἦλθε δ' Ἀμάζων, Ἄρηος θυγάτηρ, μεγαλήτορος ἀνδροφόνοιο, 'and then came the Amazon, daughter of great-hearted man-slaying Ares'. Her story was told in the *Aithiopis* of Arktinos, the lost continuation of the *Iliad*; it is doubtful whether Virgil had access to a complete text of this epic, but the story was familiar from later references and summaries and from pictorial representations.[57]

It is not clear how closely Virgil intended to identify Camilla with Penthesilea.[58] Greek Amazons were not virgins: the marriage of Theseus to the Amazon Hippolyte (also mentioned by Virgil in the Amazon

[57] For references see Comm. on 649. The only surviving epic account of Penthesilea, Quintus of Smyrna's *Fall of Troy*, is from the fourth century A.D.

[58] For further discussion of this question see Arrigoni 27–9, 55–63. There is no trace in V.'s Camilla of the idea of amazonomachy as a kind of gigantomachy, a fight against the monstrous and the barbarous, commonly found in Athenian art and literature (Arrigoni 22–3; Hardie 133–6). Virgil's concept of an idealised warrior-maid was frequently imitated in the Renaissance: see, e.g., the account of Britomart's combat with Scudamore and Artegall in Spenser, *Faerie Queene* 4.6, a passage clearly indebted to *Aen.* XI. In contrast, 'real' Amazons fight against Britomart in *F.Q.* 5.7.

simile at 11.661) is a familiar myth which survives as late as Shake-
speare's *A Midsummer Night's Dream*: Hippolyte's son Hippolytus was
identified with the Italian Virbius and is mentioned in the catalogue of
Italian chiefs (7.761–2).[59] Camilla's assumption of the role of Amazon
in book XI introduces a note of Greek fantasy into the Italian story of
the campaigns against Aeneas, though her deeds of prowess follow the
traditional epic mode and seem to balance those of Mezentius in book
X.[60] The *uenatrix–bellatrix* ambiguity remains with her throughout her
*aristeia* and perhaps helps to bring about her death. Her fatal stalking
of the priest Chloreus belongs more to the chase than to the battlefield:
she is attracted by his gorgeous gear and perhaps sees in him a narcis-
sistic self-image.[61] Her motivation remains uncertain: did she want to
dedicate the *spolia* to Diana as though they were trophies of the hunt,
or did she want to wear them herself?

There is also some ambiguity about the figure of Chloreus. He is said
to have been a former priest of Cybele. Little has been made of this.[62]
Cybele, the Great Mother of Ida, is in clear antithesis to Diana. Like
Venus, she is associated with Aeneas, who was born on Ida; he prays
to her at 10.252–5. The Italian Numanus sneered at the Trojans
('Phrygians') for their worship of Cybele, because her rites involved an
element of transexuality (9.617–20); Iarbas, too, expressed his scorn of
Aeneas' effeminate dress (4.215–17).[63] But the cult was established at
Rome as early as 204 B.C.,[64] and Virgil could safely ignore the orgiastic
element (or subsume it into enemy propaganda) and present Cybele,
like Venus, as a tutelary deity of the Trojans. (She appears at 6.784–7
in a simile illustrating the fecundity of the Roman stock.) In Lucretius'
description of the procession of the Magna Mater (*D.R.N.* 2.606–43)

[59] He is said to have been restored to life *amore Dianae*: see Fordyce on 7.761;
Fowler 79–81.

[60] Cf. M. M. Willcock, 'Battle scenes in the *Aeneid*', *P.C.P.S.* 29 (1983) 91.

[61] Cf. 11.652 and 11.774. Too much, however, can be made of sexual ambiguity in discussing both Chloreus and Camilla, e.g. by R. A. Hornsby, *Patterns of
action in the Aeneid* (Iowa 1970).

[62] The Chloreus passage is not discussed by T. P. Wiseman, 'Cybele, Virgil
and Augustus', in *Poetry and politics in the age of Augustus* ed. D. West and A.
Woodman (Cambridge 1984) 117–28. See further Cruttwell 1–12; Galinsky
224–6; Johnson 143–4.

[63] See N. Horsfall, 'I pantaloni di Cloreo', *Riv. Fil.* 116.4 (1988) 1–3.

[64] Livy 29.37.2; G. Lugli, *Roma antica* (1946) 431–2.

her priests are said to be armed and to show their willingness to fight for their native land (*ut armis | et uirtute uelint patriam defendere terram*).

After killing twelve of the enemy, Camilla dies: blindly, yet with all eyes upon her, as they were when she paraded with her fellow-chiefs at the end of book VII.[65] Everyone but she saw the arrow leave Arruns' bow and go straight to its target; she saw only Chloreus and his splendid costume. Yet her *tristis mors* becomes a transfiguration, partly through Diana's 'Homeric' rescue of her body, which is conveyed to the land of the Volsci for burial, and partly because her example inspired the *matres* of Latium to patriotic fervour. She remains in the reader's mind as the free and joyous maiden who seemed to skim land and sea as she ran, and whose name still held significance for Dante as one of those who died for Italy, enshrined in another 'catalogue' along with Nisus, Euryalus and Turnus,[66] a heroine of the Italian resistance.

We cannot hope to recover the creative process by which Camilla evolved as a character in the *Aeneid*. In book VII she is already *bellatrix* (though not Amazonian); her early life as an acolyte of Diana is not mentioned there: indeed, it is not until the hour of her death approaches that we learn, in an ecphrasis of great beauty and pathos (11.537–84),[67] of her childhood and upbringing. The words applied by Virgil to Pallas (10.508) might also serve as her own epitaph: *haec te prima dies bello dedit, haec eadem aufert.*

As for the name Camilla, it was an inspired choice.[68] The word meant a young girl employed in religious duties, as its masculine counterpart *camillus* referred to a young boy so employed. The Roman reader would have thought at once of the great Roman leader and patriot M. Furius Camillus, whose cognomen suggests that he was brought up

[65] On V.'s presentation of C. as a 'wonder to behold' (θαῦμα ἰδέσθαι) see the interesting discussion in Bonfanti 178–207.

[66] *Inferno* 1.106–8. Camilla is also mentioned by Dante in his description of Limbo (*Inferno* 4.124) along with Penthesilea, Latinus and Lavinia.

[67] On the problems raised by this passage see Comm. on 532–87.

[68] V. makes learned play with C.'s name (11.543) saying that it was a form (*mutata parte*) of the name Casmila: the kind of metonomasia, often ignoring quantity, to which he and his Hellenistic predecessors were addicted. According to Varro, *L.L.* 7.34, the Greek word κασμίλος meant an attendant of the gods, while Servius says (on 11.543) that Camillus was an Etruscan name for Mercury, minister to the gods, quoting Callimachus as his authority.

in this way.[69] He was the saviour and second founder of Rome after the Gallic invasion of 387–386 B.C., and the man who finally defeated the Volsci, whom Virgil's heroine so gallantly and hopelessly led against[70] Aeneas.

## 4. THE POETRY[71]

### (i) The Virgilian hexameter

A notable feature of Virgil's later hexameters is the increasing incidence of elision,[72] especially of long vowels and -*m*.[73] In book XI there are upwards of 500 elisions. Particularly striking are elisions in the first foot, e.g. 76 *harum unam*, 91 *hastam alii*, 94 *postquam omnis*, two successive instances at 217, 218, others at 305, 331, 438, 459, *quam* is elided in two successive vv., 308–9, and there are elisions of the first person singular verb at 503, *audeo* and *promitto* (see Comm.) and 793, *remeabo*. Other striking elisions of long vowels occur at, e.g., 515, 516, 536, 589, 843, 850, 892, 903. The frequency and boldness of such elisions has also the effect of drawing attention to passages without elision: a good example is at 76–88 (only one elision, 76) where there is also a marked and regular coincidence of ictus and stress, onomatopoeically reflecting the ordered, ritualistic disposition of the funeral rites. In contrast, vv. 352–6, part of Drances' speech, contain five elisions, as do vv. 408–10, part of Turnus' speech.

[69] Camillus is mentioned in the pageant of Roman heroes in the Elysian Fields, 6.825 *referentem signa Camillum*. Livy calls Camillus *diligentissimus religionum cultor* (5.50.1). He was said to have transferred the image of Juno from Veii, of which city she was tutelary deity, to Rome: see Livy 5.21–2; Plutarch, *Vit. Cam.* 6; Ogilvie 151.

[70] On C.'s defeat of the Volsci see Alföldi 368–77.

[71] More extended discussions may be found in, e.g., Wilkinson; Marouzeau; Camps 61–74; Quinn 350–430; Gransden, *VA* 51–75.

[72] There is more elision in the *Aeneid* than in the *Eclogues* (Soubiran 604–5) and more elision in *Aen.* XI and XII than in any other books of the poem: for full statistics see W. Ott, *Metrische Analysen zu Vergil: Aeneis Buch XI* (Tübingen 1985).

[73] Soubiran suggested (247–50) that the elision of *m* was intended to reduce the prosodic value of the *m*-syllable, which may have been unstressed or, to use his word, atonal.

The measured slowness of the funeral passage, 22–99, is secured through a higher than average incidence of predominantly spondaic verses. G. E. Duckworth distinguished sixteen possible metrical types of the regular Latin hexameter: in the present passage verses of types 4 (sdss),[74] 1 (dsss), 5 (ssss), 7 (ssds) and 13 (sssd) together account for half of the seventy lines. Lines of type 4 occur throughout book XI twice as often as lines of type 1, which is statistically the commonest type of hexameter in Virgil and Lucretius. Indeed, verses of type 4 (sdss) provide the dominant rhythm throughout the opening sequence of the book:

> et maestum Iliades crinem de more solutae.
> harum unam iuueni supremum maestus honorem.

In the following ten-line passage, spoken by Aeneas over the body of Pallas (45–54), in only three lines are dactyls conspicuous (47: dsdd; 50: sdds; 51: ddss). Of the other seven, four are of type 4 (sdss), two of type 5 (ssss) and one of type 13 (sssd):

> non haec Euandro de te promissa parenti
> discedens dederam, cum me complexus euntem
> mitteret in magnum imperium metuensque moneret
> acris esse uiros, cum dura proelia gente.
> et nunc ille quidem spe multum captus inani
> fors et uota facit cumulatque altaria donis,
> nos iuuenem exanimum et nil iam caelestibus ullis
> debentem uano maesti comitamur honore.
> infelix, nati funus crudele uidebis!
> hi nostri reditus expectatique triumphi?

Elision is employed lightly, and is mainly of -*m*; at 51, in which Aeneas reaches to the very heart of loss, *iuuenem exanimum* are both elided, as if to show how easily Pallas has slipped out of life. In this passage, with its striking alliterative patterns, language, rhythm and feeling are perfectly manipulated and represent the highest peak of Virgil's art.[75]

---

[74] For these classifications see G. E. Duckworth, *Vergil and classical hexameter poetry* (Ann Arbor, Mich. 1969). There is a summary in Gransden, *Aen. VIII*, App. B. The classification has a certain value as a means of describing the effect of different rhythms.

[75] 'In V.'s hands the long process of refinement of native resources under

## (ii) Alliteration, assonance, symmetry, repetition

Many lines and passages gain a special brilliance or pathos through alliteration. In the passage quoted above, there are particularly elaborate alliterative patterns of *p*, *d*, *c*, *m*, and *f*. Alliteration often helps to emphasise some form of symmetry, such as 'enclosing word-order'.[76] In vv. 581–4 (singled out for special admiration by Mackail)

> multae illam frustra Tyrrhena per oppida matres
> optauere nurum; sola contenta Diana
> aeternum telorum et uirginitatis amorem
> intemerata colit

581 and 583 exemplify enclosing word-order, reinforced by alliteration of the first and last words (*multae . . . matres, aeternum . . . amorem*). Further alliteration, of *t* for instance, may also be detected. The symmetry of 583 is especially notable: Similar patterns occur at, e.g., 532 *Velocem interea superis in sedibus Opim*; 589 *tristis ubi infausto committitur omine pugna*; 696 *tum ualidam perque arma uiro perque ossa securim*, where the word-order powerfully enacts the axe's violent course through the hero's armour to the very bone. Another example of alliterative symmetry with verbs (and cf. also v. 47, quoted above, section (i)) is to be found at 470 *deserit ac tristi turbatus tempore differt*, where the three central words all alliterate, as do the outer verbs. At 207–9 there is a repeated assonance of *u*, a marked alliteration of *c*, and enclosing word-order:

> cetera confusaeque ingentem caedis aceruum
> nec numero nec honore cremant; tunc undique uasti
> certatim crebris conlucent ignibus agri.

The last six words (*uasti . . . agri*) also offer a solemn spondaic rhythm.

Like most poets, Virgil is fond of word-play, which often ignores quantity, e.g. 885 *orantis, oriturque*. Word-play is combined with alliteration at 151 *et uia uix tandem uoci laxata dolore est*. At 766–7 (Arruns is

---

supervision of Greek technicians reached its acme, and the Latin language had finally been shaped into a potent and sensitive instrument of poetry' (Palmer 118).

[76] See T. E. V. Pearce, 'Enclosing word-order in the Latin hexameter', *C.Q.* n.s. 16 (1966) 140–71, 298–320.

shadowing Camilla) repetition and enclosing word-order are onomatopoeically combined with an elaborate alliterative pattern $(t, q, c)$.:

> hos aditus iamque hos aditus omnemque pererrat
> undique circuitum et certam quatit improbus hastam.

The most striking example of repetition in book XI is the recurrence of
*maestus* (in various forms of the declension, and including the cognates
*maerentes, maerentem*) throughout the first part of the book, at 26, 35, 38,
52, 76, 92, 211, 216, 226, 454, 482. These have an obvious cumulative
effect, tolling through the long account of the funeral. Repetition may
also involve the 'figura etymologica', e.g. 140 *Euandrum Euandrique*, or
it may take the form of a 'reprise', e.g. 45 *non haec Euandro de te promissa
parenti* is recalled when Evander begins his own funeral oration over
Pallas, 152 *non haec, o Palla, dederas promissa parenti*. Similarly 52 *comitamur
honore* is echoed at 61 *comitentur honorem*. Repetition at the end of successive or neighbouring lines is fairly common in the *Aeneid*: 204, 205 *partim*
(see Comm.), 618, 621 *Latini*, 173, 175 *armis*, (see Comm.), 95 *alto*,
98 *altos*, 188 *armis*, 191 *arma*.[77]

Rhyme and homoioteleuton are also fairly common in the *Aeneid*. As
Wilkinson pointed out, 'a tendency to actual rhyme could hardly fail
to occur in an inflected language, and it was promoted by the taste for
parallelism'.[78] Lines of the following type are not infrequent:

> defendentum armis aditus inque arma ruentum
> (886)

though there the rhyme is softened by elision, as also at 697:

> altior exsurgens oranti et multa precanti

and 854:

> ut uidit fulgentem armis ac uana tumentem.

---

[77] There is little evidence to support the modern view that the ancients did
not mind, or even notice, repetition: see further P. E. Easterling, *Hermes* 101
(1973) 33–4: 'repetition may not always be organised in such a way as to be
immediately recognisable as a rhetorical figure, but if it draws attention to what
is important, points a contrast or clarifies an argument, it is performing an
essentially rhetorical function'.

[78] Wilkinson 32–4; see also Austin on 4.55. Marouzeau notes (64) some
remarkable rhyme-clusters in *Aen* 2.443–64. Perhaps the most striking pair of
rhyming vv. in V. is the 'Sibylline' couplet at *Ecl.* 4.50–1.

Where there is no elision, a line rhyming at caesura and line-end is
known as a 'leonine hexameter'.[79]

Isocolia and parallelism form the basic structure of the Virgilian
sentence. The binary structure is seen at its simplest in such lines as

> hi nostri reditus expectatique triumphi
>
> (54)
>
> disiectique duces desolatique manipli
>
> (870 Comm.)
>
> it caelo clamorque uirum clangorque tubarum
>
> (192 Comm.)

or turning into the following line:

> Interea Turnum in siluis saeuissimus implet
> nuntius et iuueni ingentem fert Acca tumultum
>
> (896–7)

or with asyndeton:

> Hos inter motus, medio in flagrante tumultu.
>
> (225)

The tricolon is also very frequent, in asyndeton:

> o fortunatae gentes, Saturnia regna,
> antiqui Ausonii ...      (252–3)

with anaphora:

> Prima fugit domina amissa leuis ala Camillae,
> turbati fugiunt Rutuli, fugit acer Atinas
>
> (868–9)

or in a more complex form using both asyndeton and the copulative,
and with anaphora in the second and third cola:

> At medias inter caedes exsultat Amazon
> unum exserta latus pugnae, pharetrata Camilla,
> et nunc lenta manu spargens hastilia denset,
> nunc ualidam dextra rapit indefessa bipennem.
>
> (648–51)

---

[79] See Austin's n. on 6.622.

Longer and more elaborate structures occasionally occur, usually to create some special effect, as at 778–84 x, Camilla stalking Chloreus (see also section (iv) below), where the sense depends on, and develops from, the opening accusative (*hunc* = Chloreus, the pursued), while the rest of the material is disposed around the subject, Camilla, until in the last two lines there is a *cum*-clause carrying a change of subject, to Arruns, who will bring down Camilla. The shifting syntax reflects the shifting fortunes of war.

### (iii) Enjambment

In composing the *Aeneid*, Virgil developed a 'periodic' or paragraphic structure in which the sense is diffused through several lines in a series of linked sentences ('cola'). His syntax is generally paratactic, consisting of parallel sentences arranged in twos or threes (see above), usually linked by a copulative (especially *-que*) but sometimes arranged in asyndeton. When a 'period' or unit of discourse is completed, the sense-break often occurs within rather than at the end of a line. This is a marked feature of Virgil's later hexameters, in contradistinction to the verse of the *Eclogues*, in which end-stopped lines (the norm in Catullus' hexameters) predominate. In Catullus 64, only 40 of the poem's 408 hexameters have any appreciable pause within the line, and only two lines end in a word which is not a strong part of speech (noun, verb, or adjective), viz. 66 *passim*, 219 *nondum*.

In his first Eclogue, using Theocritus as his model, Virgil introduced a number of major sense-breaks within the line, notably the so-called 'bucolic diaeresis', sometimes combined with anaphora, thus (7–8):

> namque erit ille mihi semper deus, | illius aram
> saepe tener nostris ab ouilibus imbuet agnus.

He also used sense-breaks at other points in the verse, usually at a caesura (middle of the 2nd, 3rd or 4th foot). In the first Eclogue enjambment occurs at vv. 1, 4, 7, 9, 11, 12, 19, 20, 22, 24, 38, 42, 47, 71, 77, a ratio of roughly 1 in 5, which seems also to have accorded with the practice of Callimachus.[80] Moreover, many of these 'turns' do not

---

[80] See the analysis of the longest surviving fragment of the *Hecale* in Newman, *CET* 127.

involve full enjambment, in that, e.g. in the first two lines, although the sense is carried across the couplet each line still makes phrasal, though not clausal, sense:

> Tityre, tu patulae recubans sub tegmine fagi
> siluestrem tenui Musam meditaris auena.

Moreover, every line in the poem ends with a strong part of speech, noun, verb, adjective, or (twice only) emphatic pronoun (9 *ipsum*, 18 *nobis*).

In the *Aeneid*, however, and most markedly in the later books, Virgil allowed himself much more freedom in placing colourless or 'indifferent' words at the end of the line, thereby producing a strong enjambment. Thus in *Aeneid* I we can find *circum, ibidem, olim, ille* (twice), *ulli, si quem, si quid*. But in book XI there is a much greater incidence: 51 *ullis*, 123 *uicissim*, 164 *quas*, 170 *quam*, 201 *donec*, 204, 205 *partim*, 282, 374, 504, 873 *contra*, 283 *quantus*, 390 *istis*, 409 *isto*, 430 *quos*, 471 *ultro*, 509 *quando*, 712, 741 *ipse*, 816 *inter*, 824 *circum*. Other bold instances found in the closing books include 9.58 *atque huc*, 9.440 *atque hinc*, 12.335, 615 *atque*, 12.526 *nunc, nunc*.

Virgil continued to use the bucolic diaeresis in the *Aeneid* (in book XI at 57, 389, 550, 559). But more frequently he placed major sense-breaks at the 2nd-, 3rd- or 4th-foot caesura:

*At the 2nd-foot caesura*: 15, 92, 97, 111, 124, 237, 265, 313, 328, 380, 391 (incomplete line), 409, 424, 440, 446, 474, 698, 705, 706, 790, 792, 806, 827.
*At the 3rd-foot caesura*: 98, 120, 129, 135, 161, 166, 179, 180, 241, 282, 292, 344, 386, 399, 509, 545, 582, 584, 644, 688, 746, 747, 797, 849.
*At the 4th-foot caesura*: 143, 162, 165, 199, 208, 227, 259, 365, 366, 400, 454, 461, 501, 513, 599, 615, 640, 749, 801, 883.

Sense-breaks at the end of the first foot of the line are less frequent: 146, 309, 375 (incomplete line), 475, 549, 665, 775, 833, 857. A major sense-break in the middle of the first foot is rare: 175.

## (iv) Narrative technique

The *Aeneid* is a continuous narrative discourse. It may be necessary and convenient to break it down into small lexical or metrical units, as has been attempted in this Introduction (sections (i–iii) above) and still further in the Commentary. But the reader has also the larger and perhaps more difficult task of making connections between different parts of a long text, recognising recurring themes and images, correspondences and parallels both within the poem itself and in relation to other texts, especially those of Homer, so that the 'story' which gradually unfolds is also the presentational process itself,[81] and we may even go so far as to say, with J. K. Newman, that 'the *Aeneid* is a continuous commentary on itself'.[82] Features such as narrative transitions (marked by lexical signals such as *ecce*, *interea*), the relation between speech and action,[83] shifts of scene and perspective, variations of tempo, changes of tense – all these can only be apprehended over a large stretch of discourse.

The so-called historic or (better) narrative present is the predominant tense used in the *Aeneid*: to such an extent that it is easier to note passages in which the poet modulates into other narrative tenses, the perfect or the imperfect, often for the sake of variation but sometimes to create a special effect.[84] The perfect tense is sometimes used, in Quinn's words, 'to create a parenthesis on a different emotional level',[85] within a long sequence of present tenses. A good example of this in book XI is at 794–804, describing Apollo's response to Arruns' prayer and Camilla's death: the present tense has predominated throughout Camilla's *aristeia*, beginning at 664 *Quem telo primum, quem postremum, aspera uirgo,* | *deicis?* and is resumed at 805. Other instances of the perfect tense are at 676–7, in which the narrator pauses to comment on the deadly effectiveness of Camilla's fighting skill, and in the funeral passage 184–224 where, although the present tense predominates, the narrative modulates several times into the perfect and back again, to relax the tension and provide a longer perspective on the desolate scene.

[81] See further Gransden, *VI* 1–7.

[82] *CET* 181.

[83] See further Gransden, *VI* 185–6; R. Lanham, 'Theory of logoi: the speeches in classical and renaissance narrative', in *To tell a story* (Clark Library seminar papers, Los Angeles 1973). For statistics on the speeches in the *Aen.* see Highet 291–343.

[84] On V.'s narrative tenses see Quinn 88–97 and (a fuller discussion) Quinn, *LE* 198–238; S. Mack, *Patterns of time in Vergil* (Hamden, Conn. 1978) 33–54.

[85] *LE* 226.

The imperfect tense is also used significantly to depart from the norm of the narrative present. It may be used to describe an event which had been going on for some time, as at 100 *aderant*, and cf. 445–6 (quoted below), 534–5. A striking example of the sustained use of the imperfect occurs in the description of the priest Chloreus and Camilla's pursuit of him, 768–84, interrupting a long stretch of narrative present. In this passage there are nine imperfect tenses (and one pluperfect, 776): the tempo of the writing is, as it were, slowed down, so that we watch, as if in slow motion, the priest and his pursuer in their strange, almost ritual encounter.

In conclusion, a larger section of book XI (225–444) will be considered as a whole, in an attempt to show how the reader may engage not only with events narrated and feelings expressed (both those of the actors and also, like an undercurrent, those of the implied author) but with the presentational mode of the discourse. The first two sections of the book (1–224) have taken us through the unity of mourning towards the division of debate; only brief speeches have interrupted the narrative mode. In a swift transition, signalled by *ecce* at 226, the cut and thrust of argument displaces the sombre mood of shared grief:

> Hos inter motus, medio in flagrante tumultu,
> ecce super maesti magna Diomedis ab urbe
> legati responsa ferunt . . .

but in the key-word *maesti* the sustained note of mourning lingers on. When, in the debate which now follows, Drances says (366–7)

> sat funera fusi
> uidimus ingentis et desolauimus agros

it will not be enough to notice alliteration, assonance and spondees. The syntax itself ('we') includes the reader in a clear moment of recall: and if we turn back to the description of the burials in vv. 207–9 (quoted in section (ii) above) we see that *fusi* here echoes *confusae* there and that Drances' last four words here echo *uasti . . . agri* there. This 'recall' is the implied author's, but it is also what Drances is arguing about, the collective sense of shared grief, of shared deaths, which Turnus virtually ignores. (All Turnus will say about losses is that the other side have lost men too – the same argument that Haig used in the First World War.) Indeed, the speeches in the war-council are a dramatisation of the public conscience. People's motives are a mixture of the admitted and the repressed, the expedient and the high-minded, and the rhetoric of book XI makes a statement about the role of language itself in the conduct of human affairs.

The last speech in the debate is made by Turnus. Up to v. 409 he has been addressing Drances, angry to the point of incoherence (e.g. the ellipse of 406, see Comm.), motivated by the intense dislike of the aristocrat for the *nouus homo*. But it is with a studied show of reason that he turns to Latinus and says (410) '*nunc ad te et tua magna, pater, consulta reuertor.*' Here the word *magna* signifies 'Drances' words are of no account, but you, sir, have raised really important issues.' There follows a pair of lucid cola with *si* and the present indicative: 'If it is really true that it's all over with us, then let us sue for peace. But oh . . . ', and here a third *si*-clause, this time with the subjunctive, introduces another ellipse as emotion again takes over from reason: 'if we had any particle of our old courage left, then [I would count] that man fortunate who, before he could see such sights [our surrender] dropped down dead'. The perfect indicatives generalise Turnus' rhetoric. Hypothesis and reality become confused. Another pair of *cola* with *sin* and the indicative now follows: 'But if on the other hand . . . ' Logic now reasserts itself. 'If we still have allies in reserve, if [it is true that] the Trojan victory has been won at a heavy cost, then what are we waiting for?' Turnus the emotional epic hero is replaced by Turnus the practical strategist. But there now follow three lines of philosophic generalisation about human affairs (425–7) whose dependence on Ennius gives them a vaguely reassuring ring, but in fact this is mere gambler's philosophy: the next throw of the dice may change one's luck. After these three lines, Turnus' strategic indecisiveness becomes evident. 'We have plenty of reserves, including Camilla and her Volsci; but if (*quod si . . .*) I am really such an obstacle to the common good and I must face Aeneas alone, I shall do so, even though he should surpass Achilles in his divine armour.' These last lines are intended to inspire his hearers with confidence; the strong, emphatic first-person singulars are characteristically self-vaunting (*ibo animis contra . . . Turnus ego . . . deuoui . . . oro*). The final couplet of the speech reverts to obscure but fine-sounding aphorism; it is enough for Turnus, and, he hopes, his hearers, that the words *uirtus et gloria* ring out, and that he should win them, not Drances, who is now mentioned for the first time since 409.

After the debate there is another transitional passage using the imperfect tense (see above) before the war resumes (445–8):

> Illi haec inter se dubiis de rebus agebant
> certantes: castra Aeneas aciemque mouebat.
> nuntius ingenti per regia tecta tumultu
> ecce ruit . . .

These lines echo 225–8 (quoted above): cf. *haec inter* (*Hos inter*), *tumultu*, *ecce*, *nuntius* (*legati*). Now the women of Italy pray to Athene to help them against Aeneas; the goddess and her female worshippers prepare us for Camilla: the repeated *uirgo . . . uirgo* (479, 483) refers to Lavinia and Athene, but it anticipates the repeated use of the word at 557, 664, 676, to refer to Diana and Camilla.

## NOTE ON THE TEXT

The text used is that of Oxford Classical Texts, *Vergili Opera* (revised 1990), reprinted by permission of Oxford University Press. The following changes have been made: at 149 *Pallanta* for *Pallante*, and at 173 *armis* for *aruis*: these are discussed in the Commentary. In addition, the punctuation has been changed at vv. 18, 373, 415, 643, 684, 734 and 737; additional new paragraphs have been marked at 410, 567.

# P. VERGILI MARONIS
# AENEIDOS LIBER VNDECIMVS

# SIGLA

| | | |
|---|---|---|
| *F* | Vaticanus lat. 3225 | saec. iv |
| *M* | Florentinus Laur. xxxix. 1 | saec. v |
| *P* | Vaticanus Palatinus lat. 1631 | saec. iv/v |
| *R* | Vaticanus lat. 3867 | saec. v |
| *V* | fragmenta Veronensia | saec. v |
| *M²P²R²* | corrector aliquis antiquus | |

*Codices saeculi noni*:

| | |
|---|---|
| *a* | Bernensis 172 cum Parisino lat. 7929 |
| *b* | Bernensis 165 |
| *c* | Bernensis 184 |
| *d* | Bernensis 255 + 239 |
| *e* | Bernensis 167 |
| *f* | Oxoniensis Bodl. Auct. F. 2. 8 |
| *h* | Valentianensis 407 |
| *r* | Parisinus lat. 7926 |
| *t* | Parisinus lat. 13043 |
| *u* | Parisinus lat. 13044 |
| *v* | Vaticanus lat. 1570 |
| ω | consensus horum uel omnium uel quotquot non separatim nominantur |
| γ | Guelferbytanus Gudianus lat. 2°. 70 |
| *def.* | deficit (uel mutilus est uel legi non potest) |
| *recc.* | codices saec. nono recentiores |

Oceanum interea surgens Aurora reliquit:
Aeneas, quamquam et sociis dare tempus humandis
praecipitant curae turbataque funere mens est,
uota deum primo uictor soluebat Eoo.
ingentem quercum decisis undique ramis                     5
constituit tumulo fulgentiaque induit arma,
Mezenti ducis exuuias, tibi magne tropaeum
bellipotens; aptat rorantis sanguine cristas
telaque trunca uiri, et bis sex thoraca petitum
perfossumque locis, clipeumque ex aere sinistrae          10
subligat atque ensem collo suspendit eburnum.
tum socios (namque omnis eum stipata tegebat
turba ducum) sic incipiens hortatur ouantis:
'maxima res effecta, uiri; timor omnis abesto,
quod superest; haec sunt spolia et de rege superbo        15
primitiae manibusque meis Mezentius hic est.
nunc iter ad regem nobis murosque Latinos.
arma parate animis et spe praesumite bellum,
ne qua mora ignaros, ubi primum uellere signa
adnuerint superi pubemque educere castris,                20
impediat segnisue metu sententia tardet.
interea socios inhumataque corpora terrae
mandemus, qui solus honos Acheronte sub imo est.
ite,' ait 'egregias animas, quae sanguine nobis
hanc patriam peperere suo, decorate supremis              25
muneribus, maestamque Euandri primus ad urbem
mittatur Pallas, quem non uirtutis egentem
abstulit atra dies et funere mersit acerbo.'

1–28 MPR    21 segnisue M¹R: -que M²Pω(sig-Pcr)    23 est Mω, Tib.: om.
PR    24 qui Macrob. 4.4.9

Sic ait inlacrimans, recipitque ad limina gressum
corpus ubi exanimi positum Pallantis Acoetes     30
seruabat senior, qui Parrhasio Euandro
armiger ante fuit, sed non felicibus aeque
tum comes auspiciis caro datus ibat alumno.
circum omnis famulumque manus Troianaque turba
et maestum Iliades crinem de more solutae.     35
ut uero Aeneas foribus sese intulit altis
ingentem gemitum tunsis ad sidera tollunt
pectoribus, maestoque immugit regia luctu.
ipse caput niuei fultum Pallantis et ora
ut uidit leuique patens in pectore uulnus     40
cuspidis Ausoniae, lacrimis ita fatur obortis:
'tene,' inquit 'miserande puer, cum laeta ueniret,
inuidit Fortuna mihi, ne regna uideres
nostra neque ad sedes uictor ueherere paternas?
non haec Euandro de te promissa parenti     45
discedens dederam, cum me complexus euntem
mitteret in magnum imperium metuensque moneret
acris esse uiros, cum dura proelia gente.
et nunc ille quidem spe multum captus inani
fors et uota facit cumulatque altaria donis,     50
nos iuuenem exanimum et nil iam caelestibus ullis
debentem uano maesti comitamur honore.
infelix, nati funus crudele uidebis!
hi nostri reditus exspectatique triumphi?
haec mea magna fides? at non, Euandre, pudendis     55
uulneribus pulsum aspicies, nec sospite dirum
optabis nato funus pater. ei mihi quantum
praesidium, Ausonia, et quantum tu perdis, Iule!'
    Haec ubi defleuit, tolli miserabile corpus
imperat, et toto lectos ex agmine mittit     60

29–60 *MPR*     30 exanimis *Rceuv*     41 abortis *ceuv*     42 ten *Mar. Vict.*
22.9     51 exanimem *Rceuv*     54 exoptatique *R*     57 ei *MPb*: et *R*, *Tib.*: heu
ω     60 agmine *Mω, Seru.*: ordine (*cf. A.* 7.152) *PR*

mille uiros qui supremum comitentur honorem
intersintque patris lacrimis, solacia luctus
exigua ingentis, misero sed debita patri.
haud segnes alii cratis et molle feretrum
arbuteis texunt uirgis et uimine querno                    65
exstructosque toros obtentu frondis inumbrant.
hic iuuenem agresti sublimem stramine ponunt:
qualem uirgineo demessum pollice florem
seu mollis uiolae seu languentis hyacinthi,
cui neque fulgor adhuc nec dum sua forma recessit,        70
non iam mater alit tellus uirisque ministrat.
tum geminas uestis auroque ostroque rigentis
extulit Aeneas, quas illi laeta laborum
ipsa suis quondam manibus Sidonia Dido
fecerat et tenui telas discreuerat auro.                  75
harum unam iuueni supremum maestus honorem
induit arsurasque comas obnubit amictu,
multaque praeterea Laurentis praemia pugnae
aggerat et longo praedam iubet ordine duci;
addit equos et tela quibus spoliauerat hostem.           80
uinxerat et post terga manus, quos mitteret umbris
inferias, caeso sparsurus sanguine flammas,
indutosque iubet truncos hostilibus armis
ipsos ferre duces inimicaque nomina figi.
ducitur infelix aeuo confectus Acoetes,                   85
pectora nunc foedans pugnis, nunc unguibus ora,
sternitur et toto proiectus corpore terrae;
ducunt et Rutulo perfusos sanguine currus.
post bellator equus positis insignibus Aethon
it lacrimans guttisque umectat grandibus ora.            90
hastam alii galeamque ferunt, nam cetera Turnus
uictor habet. tum maesta phalanx Teucrique sequuntur

---

61–92 *MPR*    82 sparsuros ω (*praeter r*), agnoscit *Tib.*    flammam *R*    84
fingi *R*

Tyrrhenique omnes et uersis Arcades armis.
postquam omnis longe comitum praecesserat ordo,
substitit Aeneas gemituque haec addidit alto:                    95
'nos alias hinc ad lacrimas eadem horrida belli
fata uocant: salue aeternum mihi, maxime Palla,
aeternumque uale.' nec plura effatus ad altos
tendebat muros gressumque in castra ferebat.
    Iamque oratores aderant ex urbe Latina                       100
uelati ramis oleae ueniamque rogantes:
corpora, per campos ferro quae fusa iacebant,
redderet ac tumulo sineret succedere terrae;
nullum cum uictis certamen et aethere cassis;
parceret hospitibus quondam socerisque uocatis.                  105
quos bonus Aeneas haud aspernanda precantis
prosequitur uenia et uerbis haec insuper addit:
'quaenam uos tanto fortuna indigna, Latini,
implicuit bello, qui nos fugiatis amicos?
pacem me exanimis et Martis sorte peremptis                      110
oratis? equidem et uiuis concedere uellem.
nec ueni, nisi fata locum sedemque dedissent,
nec bellum cum gente gero; rex nostra reliquit
hospitia et Turni potius se credidit armis.
aequius huic Turnum fuerat se opponere morti.                    115
si bellum finire manu, si pellere Teucros
apparat, his mecum decuit concurrere telis:
uixet cui uitam deus aut sua dextra dedisset.
nunc ite et miseris supponite ciuibus ignem.'
dixerat Aeneas. illi obstipuere silentes                         120
conuersique oculos inter se atque ora tenebant.
    Tum senior semperque odiis et crimine Drances
infensus iuueni Turno sic ore uicissim
orsa refert: 'o fama ingens, ingentior armis,

93–124 MPR    93 omnes MPcfhrv: duces (u. 171) Rbdeu, Seru.    95 edidit
M²Reu    101 rogantes MPω: precantes Reu, Seru. ad A. 10.31    104 aere
dfh    110 pacem me] pacemne cdeuv    113 relinquit eu    117 decuit
mecum cdfh    118 sua] cui P²

uir Troiane, quibus caelo te laudibus aequem?          125
iustitiaene prius mirer belline laborum?
nos uero haec patriam grati referemus ad urbem
et te, si qua uiam dederit Fortuna, Latino
iungemus regi. quaerat sibi foedera Turnus.
quin et fatalis murorum attollere moles          130
saxaque subuectare umeris Troiana iuuabit.'
dixerat haec unoque omnes eadem ore fremebant.
bis senos pepigere dies, et pace sequestra
per siluas Teucri mixtique impune Latini
errauere iugis. ferro sonat alta bipenni          135
fraxinus, euertunt actas ad sidera pinus,
robora nec cuneis et olentem scindere cedrum
nec plaustris cessant uectare gementibus ornos.

Et iam Fama uolans, tanti praenuntia luctus,
Euandrum Euandrique domos et moenia replet,          140
quae modo uictorem Latio Pallanta ferebat.
Arcades ad portas ruere et de more uetusto
funereas rapuere faces; lucet uia longo
ordine flammarum et late discriminat agros.
contra turba Phrygum ueniens plangentia iungit          145
agmina. quae postquam matres succedere tectis
uiderunt, maestam incendunt clamoribus urbem.
at non Euandrum potis est uis ulla tenere,
sed uenit in medios. feretro Pallanta reposto
procubuit super atque haeret lacrimansque gemensque,          150
et uia uix tandem uoci laxata dolore est:
'non haec, o Palla, dederas promissa parenti,
cautius ut saeuo uelles te credere Marti.
haud ignarus eram quantum noua gloria in armis

---

125–54 *MPR*     126 iustitiaene *Pω*, 'inuenitur etiam' teste *Prisc.* 17.102: -iane *MR*,
*Prisc. saepius*, agnoscit *D Seru.*: -iamne *r*     laborem *P¹Rr*     131 subiectare *P¹*:
subuectari *cd*     134 siluam *M*     140 conplet *M²*     142 at portis 'multa
exemplaria' ap. *D Seru.*     145 iungunt *Mbr*     149 Pallanta *M²*: Pallante *PR
ωγ, Seru.*     150 procumbit *R*     151 uoci *M²* (uoces *M¹*) *P¹Rω*: uocis *P²*
152 petenti 'alii' ap. *D Seru.*

et praedulce decus primo certamine posset.                    155
primitiae iuuenis miserae bellique propinqui
dura rudimenta, et nulli exaudita deorum
uota precesque meae! tuque, o sanctissima coniunx,
felix morte tua neque in hunc seruata dolorem!
contra ego uiuendo uici mea fata, superstes              160
restarem ut genitor. Troum socia arma secutum
obruerent Rutuli telis! animam ipse dedissem
atque haec pompa domum me, non Pallanta, referret!
nec uos arguerim, Teucri, nec foedera nec quas
iunximus hospitio dextras: sors ista senectae              165
debita erat nostrae. quod si immatura manebat
mors gnatum, caesis Volscorum milibus ante
ducentem in Latium Teucros cecidisse iuuabit.
quin ego non alio digner te funere, Palla,
quam pius Aeneas et quam magni Phryges et quam       170
Tyrrhenique duces, Tyrrhenum exercitus omnis.
magna tropaea ferunt quos dat tua dextera leto;
tu quoque nunc stares immanis truncus in armis,
esset par aetas et idem si robur ab annis,
Turne. sed infelix Teucros quid demoror armis?         175
uadite et haec memores regi mandata referte:
quod uitam moror inuisam Pallante perempto
dextera causa tua est, Turnum gnatoque patrique
quam debere uides. meritis uacat hic tibi solus
fortunaeque locus. non uitae gaudia quaero,              180
nec fas, sed gnato manis perferre sub imos.'
   Aurora interea miseris mortalibus almam
extulerat lucem referens opera atque labores:
iam pater Aeneas, iam curuo in litore Tarchon
constituere pyras. huc corpora quisque suorum             185
more tulere patrum, subiectisque ignibus atris

155–86 MPR    164 arguerim Ru    168 iuuabit Pω, Seru.: iuuaret Mb?r?,
Tib.: iuuare R    169 dignem 'alii' ap. D Seru.    172 ferant Pbd    173 armis
codd. (cf. A. 7.430): aruis Bentley    175 armis] ultra N. Heinsius    176 audite
P¹R

conditur in tenebras altum caligine caelum.
ter circum accensos cincti fulgentibus armis
decurrere rogos, ter maestum funeris ignem
lustrauere in equis ululatusque ore dedere.                    190
spargitur et tellus lacrimis, sparguntur et arma,
it caelo clamorque uirum clangorque tubarum.
hic alii spolia occisis derepta Latinis
coniciunt igni, galeas ensisque decoros
frenaque feruentisque rotas; pars munera nota,      195
ipsorum clipeos et non felicia tela.
multa boum circa mactantur corpora Morti,
saetigerosque sues raptasque ex omnibus agris
in flammam iugulant pecudes, tum litore toto
ardentis spectant socios semustaque seruant      200
busta, neque auelli possunt, nox umida donec
inuertit caelum stellis ardentibus aptum.

     Nec minus et miseri diuersa in parte Latini
innumeras struxere pyras, et corpora partim
multa uirum terrae infodiunt, auectaque partim      205
finitimos tollunt in agros urbique remittunt.
cetera confusaeque ingentem caedis aceruum
nec numero nec honore cremant; tunc undique uasti
certatim crebris conlucent ignibus agri.
tertia lux gelidam caelo dimouerat umbram:      210
maerentes altum cinerem et confusa ruebant
ossa focis tepidoque onerabant aggere terrae.
iam uero in tectis, praediuitis urbe Latini,
praecipuus fragor et longi pars maxima luctus.
hic matres miseraeque nurus, hic cara sororum      215
pectora maerentum puerique parentibus orbi
dirum exsecrantur bellum Turnique hymenaeos;
ipsum armis ipsumque iubent decernere ferro,

---

187–218 *MPR*     202 ardentibus (*A.* 4.482, 6.797) *MP*ω: fulgentibus (*cf. Macrob.* 6.1.9) *Reu, proper* ardentis (*u.* 200) *non male*     207 caedis] stragis (*A.* 6.504, 11.384) *Reu*     208 nec (*2°*)] neque *P*     214 longe ω, '*melius*' iudice Seru.

qui regnum Italiae et primos sibi poscat honores.
ingrauat haec saeuus Drances solumque uocari          220
testatur, solum posci in certamine Turnum.
multa simul contra uariis sententia dictis
pro Turno, et magnum reginae nomen obumbrat,
multa uirum meritis sustentat fama tropaeis.

Hos inter motus, medio in flagrante tumultu,          225
ecce super maesti magna Diomedis ab urbe
legati responsa ferunt: nihil omnibus actum
tantorum impensis operum, nil dona neque aurum
nec magnas ualuisse preces, alia arma Latinis
quaerenda, aut pacem Troiano ab rege petendum.          230
deficit ingenti luctu rex ipse Latinus:
fatalem Aenean manifesto numine ferri
admonet ira deum tumulique ante ora recentes.
ergo concilium magnum primosque suorum
imperio accitos alta intra limina cogit.          235
olli conuenere fluuntque ad regia plenis
tecta uiis. sedet in mediis et maximus aeuo
et primus sceptris haud laeta fronte Latinus.
atque hic legatos Aetola ex urbe remissos
quae referant fari iubet, et responsa reposcit          240
ordine cuncta suo. tum facta silentia linguis,
et Venulus dicto parens ita farier infit:
'Vidimus, o ciues, Diomedem Argiuaque castra,
atque iter emensi casus superauimus omnis,
contigimusque manum qua concidit Ilia tellus.          245
ille urbem Argyripam patriae cognomine gentis
uictor Gargani condebat Iapygis agris.
postquam introgressi et coram data copia fandi,

219–48 MPR          220 haec] et P          221 certamine Reuv          224 uirum] simul
(u. 222) M¹          226 magni (A. 8.9) agnoscit Seru.          228 nec Rω(praeter cv),
Tib.          230 petendum M²bhu, Seru. hic et ad A.10.628, DSeru. ad G. 4.484:
petendam M²PRω          235 limina] moenia Reu          236 olli] ilico df  ruuntque
Mbr          243 Diomedem cdhu: -den MPRbe, Tib.: -de f, agnoscit Seru. (cf. Macrob.
5.17.19)          247 aruis (A. 10.390) dfhv, Seru., Tib.          248 congressi Reu, Tib.

munera praeferimus, nomen patriamque docemus,
qui bellum intulerint, quae causa attraxerit Arpos.           250
auditis ille haec placido sic reddidit ore:
"o fortunatae gentes, Saturnia regna,
antiqui Ausonii, quae uos fortuna quietos
sollicitat suadetque ignota lacessere bella?
quicumque Iliacos ferro uiolauimus agros                      255
(mitto ea quae muris bellando exhausta sub altis,
quos Simois premat ille uiros) infanda per orbem
supplicia et scelerum poenas expendimus omnes,
uel Priamo miseranda manus; scit triste Mineruae
sidus et Euboicae cautes ultorque Caphereus.                  260
militia ex illa diuersum ad litus abacti
Atrides Protei Menelaus adusque columnas
exsulat, Aetnaeos uidit Cyclopas Vlixes.
regna Neoptolemi referam uersosque penatis
Idomenei? Libycone habitantis litore Locros?                  265
ipse Mycenaeus magnorum ductor Achiuum
coniugis infandae prima inter limina dextra
oppetiit, deuictam Asiam subsedit adulter.
inuidisse deos, patriis ut redditus aris
coniugium optatum et pulchram Calydona uiderem?               270
nunc etiam horribili uisu portenta sequuntur
et socii amissi petierunt aethera pennis
fluminibusque uagantur aues (heu, dira meorum
supplicia!) et scopulos lacrimosis uocibus implent.
haec adeo ex illo mihi iam speranda fuerunt                   275
tempore cum ferro caelestia corpora demens
appetii et Veneris uiolaui uulnere dextram.
ne uero, ne me ad talis impellite pugnas.

---

249–78 *MPR*     251 edidit (*A.* 7.194) *M²*     255 populauimus *Reu*     258
sceleris . . . omnis '*alii*' *ap. Seru.*     259 manus] damus *P²*, *agnoscit Tib.*     267
inter *Pcrv*, *Macrob.* 4.3.12, *Tib.*: intra *MRω* (*cf. u* 882), *Seru.*     268 deuicta Asia
*defhuv*, '*melius*' *iudice Seru.*     subsedit *M¹ Pω*, *Seru.*: possedit *M²R*, *Macrob.* 4.4.22,
*Tib.*     272 amissis *P¹*: admissis '*nonnulli*' *ap: Seru.*     275 adeo] eadem *P*     ex
illo *om. R*

nec mihi cum Teucris ullum post eruta bellum
Pergama nec ueterum memini laetorue malorum.     280
munera quae patriis ad me portatis ab oris
uertite ad Aenean. stetimus tela aspera contra
contulimusque manus: experto credite quantus
in clipeum adsurgat, quo turbine torqueat hastam.
si duo praeterea talis Idaea tulisset     285
terra uiros, ultro Inachias uenisset ad urbes
Dardanus, et uersis lugeret Graecia fatis.
quidquid apud durae cessatum est moenia Troiae,
Hectoris Aeneaeque manu uictoria Graium
haesit et in decimum uestigia rettulit annum.     290
ambo animis, ambo insignes praestantibus armis,
hic pietate prior. coeant in foedera dextrae,
qua datur; ast armis concurrant arma cauete.''
et responsa simul quae sint, rex optime, regis
audisti et quae sit magno sententia bello.'     295
Vix ea legati, uariusque per ora cucurrit
Ausonidum turbata fremor, ceu saxa morantur
cum rapidos amnis, fit clauso gurgite murmur
uicinaeque fremunt ripae crepitantibus undis.
ut primum placati animi et trepida ora quierunt,     300
praefatus diuos solio rex infit ab alto:
'Ante equidem summa de re statuisse, Latini,
et uellem et fuerat melius, non tempore tali
cogere concilium, cum muros adsidet hostis.
bellum importunum, ciues, cum gente deorum     305
inuictisque uiris gerimus, quos nulla fatigant
proelia nec uicti possunt absistere ferro.
spem si quam ascitis Aetolum habuistis in armis,
ponite. spes sibi quisque; sed haec quam angusta uidetis.
cetera qua rerum iaceant perculsa ruina,     310

---

279–310 MPR     279 diruta R    bellum MPr: bellum est Rω     281 portastis
ω(praeter rv), Seru.     288 certatum M²     304 obsidet Mbrv

ante oculos interque manus sunt omnia uestras.
nec quemquam incuso: potuit quae plurima uirtus
esse, fuit; toto certatum est corpore regni.
nunc adeo quae sit dubiae sententia menti,
expediam et paucis (animos adhibete) docebo.          315
est antiquus ager Tusco mihi proximus amni,
longus in occasum, finis super usque Sicanos;
Aurunci Rutulique serunt, et uomere duros
exercent collis atque horum asperrima pascunt.
haec omnis regio et celsi plaga pinea montis          320
cedat amicitiae Teucrorum, et foederis aequas
dicamus leges sociosque in regna uocemus:
considant, si tantus amor, et moenia condant.
sin alios finis aliamque capessere gentem
est animus possuntque solo decedere nostro,           325
bis denas Italo texamus robore nauis;
seu pluris complere ualent, iacet omnis ad undam
materies: ipsi numerumque modumque carinis
praecipiant, nos aera, manus, naualia demus.
praeterea, qui dicta ferant et foedera firment         330
centum oratores prima de gente Latinos
ire placet pacisque manu praetendere ramos,
munera portantis aurique eborisque talenta
et sellam regni trabeamque insignia nostri
consulite in medium et rebus succurrite fessis.'       335
  Tum Drances idem infensus, quem gloria Turni
obliqua inuidia stimulisque agitabat amaris,
largus opum et lingua melior, sed frigida bello
dextera, consiliis habitus non futtilis auctor,
seditione potens (genus huic materna superbum          340
nobilitas dabat, incertum de patre ferebat),
surgit et his onerat dictis atque aggerat iras:

311–42 MPR    315 et del. P²    324 aliamque MRdfhr: -ue Pω, Tib
fessis] uestris P    338 linguae P¹, DSeru. (collato A. 1.441 umbrae)
ferebat MP²ω: ferebant P¹Rc

'rem nulli obscuram nostrae nec uocis egentem  
consulis, o bone rex: cuncti se scire fatentur  
quid fortuna ferat populi, sed dicere mussant.      345  
det libertatem fandi flatusque remittat,  
cuius ob auspicium infaustum moresque sinistros  
(dicam equidem, licet arma mihi mortemque minetur)  
lumina tot cecidisse ducum totamque uidemus  
consedisse urbem luctu, cum Troia temptat      350  
castra fugae fidens et caelum territat armis.  
unum etiam donis istis, quae plurima mitti  
Dardanidis dicique iubes, unum, optime regum,  
adicias, nec te ullius uiolentia uincat  
quin natam egregio genero dignisque hymenaeis      355  
des pater, et pacem hanc aeterno foedere iungas.  
quod si tantus habet mentes et pectora terror,  
ipsum obtestemur ueniamque oremus ab ipso:  
cedat, ius proprium regi patriaeque remittat.  
quid miseros totiens in aperta pericula ciuis      360  
proicis, o Latio caput horum et causa malorum?  
nulla salus bello, pacem te poscimus omnes,  
Turne, simul pacis solum inuiolabile pignus.  
primus ego, inuisum quem tu tibi fingis (et esse  
nil moror), en supplex uenio. miserere tuorum,      365  
pone animos et pulsus abi. sat funera fusi  
uidimus ingentis et desolauimus agros.  
aut, si fama mouet, si tantum pectore robur  
concipis et si adeo dotalis regia cordi est,  
aude atque aduersum fidens fer pectus in hostem.      370  
scilicet ut Turno contingat regia coniunx,  
nos animae uiles, inhumata infletaque turba,  
sternamur campis? etiam tu, si qua tibi uis,

---

343–73 *MPR*      345 ferat *M²PRbr*, *Tib.*: petat *M¹ω*      356 iungas (*A*. 8.56 *al.*) *M¹Pω*: firmes (*u.* 330) *M²Rr*      366 funere *P*   fusi *M²Rω*, *Seru.*: fusis *M¹*: fuso *P*      367 designauimus *Pb*?      369 et] aut *M*      373 sternemur *cefhuv*, *Tib.*

si patri quid Martis habes, illum aspice contra
qui uocat.' 375
  Talibus exarsit dictis uiolentia Turni.
dat gemitum rumpitque has imo pectore uoces:
'larga quidem semper, Drance, tibi copia fandi
tum cum bella manus poscunt, patribusque uocatis
primus ades. sed non replenda est curia uerbis, 380
quae tuto tibi magna uolant, dum distinet hostem
agger murorum nec inundant sanguine fossae.
proinde tona eloquio (solitum tibi) meque timoris
argue tu, Drance, quando tot stragis aceruos
Teucrorum tua dextra dedit, passimque tropaeis 385
insignis agros. possit quid uiuida uirtus
experiare licet, nec longe scilicet hostes
quaerendi nobis; circumstant undique muros.
imus in aduersos – quid cessas? an tibi Mauors
uentosa in lingua pedibusque fugacibus istis 390
semper erit?
  pulsus ego? aut quisquam merito, foedissime, pulsum
arguet, Iliaco tumidum qui crescere Thybrim
sanguine et Euandri totam cum stirpe uidebit
procubuisse domum atque exutos Arcadas armis? 395
haud ita me experti Bitias et Pandarus ingens
et quos mille die uictor sub Tartara misi,
inclusus muris hostilique aggere saeptus.
nulla salus bello? capiti cane talia, demens,
Dardanio rebusque tuis. proinde omnia magno 400
ne cessa turbare metu atque extollere uiris
gentis bis uictae, contra premere arma Latini.
nunc et Myrmidonum proceres Phrygia arma tremescunt,
nunc et Tydides et Larisaeus Achilles,

374–404 MPR    378 Drance semper M    381 distinet Pω, Seru.: detinet M:
destinat R    382 agger r, Prisc. 8.26: aggere MPRω (cf. A. 10.144)   nec] et
P    fossas (A. 10.24) Prisc., 'inuenitur tamen in quibusdam codd.' fossae    391
nequiquam armis terrebimus hostem add. M¹, del. M²    393 arguit M¹

amnis et Hadriacas retro fugit Aufidus undas.                    405
uel cum se pauidum contra mea iurgia fingit,
artificis scelus, et formidine crimen acerbat.
numquam animam talem dextra hac (absiste moueri)
amittes: habitet tecum et sit pectore in isto.
    Nunc ad te et tua magna, pater, consulta reuertor.           410
si nullam nostris ultra spem ponis in armis,
si tam deserti sumus et semel agmine uerso
funditus occidimus neque habet Fortuna regressum,
oremus pacem et dextras tendamus inertis.
quamquam o si solitae quicquam uirtutis adesset,               415
ille mihi ante alios fortunatusque laborum
egregiusque animi, qui, ne quid tale uideret,
procubuit moriens et humum semel ore momordit.
sin et opes nobis et adhuc intacta iuuentus
auxilioque urbes Italae populique supersunt,                    420
sin et Troianis cum multo gloria uenit
sanguine (sunt illis sua funera, parque per omnis
tempestas), cur indecores in limine primo
deficimus? cur ante tubam tremor occupat artus?
multa dies uariique labor mutabilis aeui                        425
rettulit in melius, multos alterna reuisens
lusit et in solido rursus Fortuna locauit.
non erit auxilio nobis Aetolus et Arpi:
at Messapus erit felixque Tolumnius et quos
tot populi misere duces, nec parua sequetur                     430
gloria delectos Latio et Laurentibus agris.
est et Volscorum egregia de gente Camilla
agmen agens equitum et florentis aere cateruas.
quod si me solum Teucri in certamina poscunt
idque placet tantumque bonis communibus obsto,                  435
non adeo has exosa manus Victoria fugit

---

405–36 MPR    410 magna PRch: magne Mω, Tib.    412 semel] simul
P    418 semel M²ω, Seru., Tib.: semul P: simul M¹R    422 suntque Rb    illis]
'legitur et illi' Seru.    425 uariusque M²P²ceruv, Macrob. 6.2.16, Non. 380.40
426 multosque M²    430 parua] tarda (G. 2.52) Seru.    431 deiectos bfhuv

ut tanta quicquam pro spe temptare recusem,
ibo animis contra, uel magnum praestet Achillem
factaque Volcani manibus paria induat arma
ille licet. uobis animam hanc soceroque Latino
Turnus ego, haud ulli ueterum uirtute secundus,          440
deuoui. solum Aeneas uocat? et uocet oro;
nec Drances potius, siue est haec ira deorum,
morte luat, siue est uirtus et gloria, tollat.'

    Illi haec inter se dubiis de rebus agebant
certantes: castra Aeneas aciemque mouebat.              445
nuntius ingenti per regia tecta tumultu
ecce ruit magnisque urbem terroribus implet:
instructos acie Tiberino a flumine Teucros
Tyrrhenamque manum totis descendere campis.
extemplo turbati animi concussaque uulgi              450
pectora et arrectae stimulis haud mollibus irae.
arma manu trepidi poscunt, fremit arma iuuentus,
flent maesti mussantque patres. hic undique clamor
dissensu uario magnus se tollit in auras,
haud secus atque alto in luco cum forte cateruae       455
consedere auium, piscosoue amne Padusae
dant sonitum rauci per stagna loquacia cycni.
'immo,' ait 'o ciues,' arrepto tempore Turnus,
'cogite concilium et pacem laudate sedentes;           460
illi armis in regna ruunt.' nec plura locutus
corripuit sese et tectis citus extulit altis.
'tu, Voluse, armari Volscorum edice maniplis,
duc' ait 'et Rutulos. equitem Messapus in armis,
et cum fratre Coras latis diffundite campis.           465
pars aditus urbis firment turrisque capessant;
cetera, qua iusso, mecum manus inferat arma.'
    Ilicet in muros tota discurritur urbe.

437–68 MPR     439 induit (A. 9.180, 11.6) P     451 animo Reu     455 in]
ad M     461 ruant e recc. N. Heinsius     463 maniplos P     464 equitem (ut
A. 10.239, 11.517) MP¹buh, Asper 534.21, Seru.: equites P²Rω, Cledon. 44.15
466 firment M¹Rω: firmet M²P     capessant Rω: capessat MP

concilium ipse pater et magna incepta Latinus
deserit ac tristi turbatus tempore differt,                          470
multaque se incusat qui non acceperit ultro
Dardanium Aenean generumque asciuerit urbi.
praefodiunt alii portas aut saxa sudesque
subuectant. bello dat signum rauca cruentum
bucina. tum muros uaria cinxere corona                               475
matronae puerique, uocat labor ultimus omnis.
nec non ad templum summasque ad Palladis arces
subuehitur magna matrum regina caterua
dona ferens, iuxtaque comes Lauinia uirgo,
causa mali tanti, oculos deiecta decoros.                            480
succedunt matres et templum ture uaporant
et maestas alto fundunt de limine uoces:
'armipotens, praeses belli, Tritonia uirgo,
frange manu telum Phrygii praedonis, et ipsum
pronum sterne solo portisque effunde sub altis.'                     485
cingitur ipse furens certatim in proelia Turnus.
iamque adeo rutilum thoraca indutus aënis
horrebat squamis surasque incluserat auro,
tempora nudus adhuc, laterique accinxerat ensem,
fulgebatque alta decurrens aureus arce                               490
exsultatque animis et spe iam praecipit hostem:
qualis ubi abruptis fugit praesepia uinclis
tandem liber equus, campoque potitus aperto
aut ille in pastus armentaque tendit equarum
aut adsuetus aquae perfundi flumine noto                             495
emicat, arrectisque fremit ceruicibus alte
luxurians luduntque iubae per colla, per armos.
  Obuia cui Volscorum acie comitante Camilla
occurrit portisque ab equo regina sub ipsis

---

469–499 MPR      469 consilium pater ipse M¹      471 qui] quod P²    ultro]
fortasse ante (A. 12.612)      472 urbi] fort. ultro (12.613)      480 mali tanti (A.
6.93) M²Pfr, Seru. (mali tantis M¹b): malis tantis Rω, agnoscit Tib.      483
praeses M¹P¹Rdr: praesens M²P²ω, Macrob. 5.3.10, agnoscit DSeru.      487
rutilum Rbr: Rutulum MPω, Tib.

desiluit, quam tota cohors imitata relictis 500
ad terram defluxit equis; tum talia fatur:
'Turne, sui merito si qua est fiducia forti,
audeo et Aeneadum promitto occurrere turmae
solaque Tyrrhenos equites ire obuia contra.
me sine prima manu temptare pericula belli, 505
tu pedes ad muros subsiste et moenia serua.'
Turnus ad haec oculos horrenda in uirgine fixus:
'o decus Italiae uirgo, quas dicere grates
quasue referre parem? sed nunc, est omnia quando
iste animus supra, mecum partire laborem. 510
Aeneas, ut fama fidem missique reportant
exploratores, equitum leuia improbus arma
praemisit, quaterent campos; ipse ardua montis
per deserta iugo superans aduentat ad urbem.
furta paro belli conuexo in tramite siluae, 515
ut biuias armato obsidam milite fauces.
tu Tyrrhenum equitem conlatis excipe signis;
tecum acer Messapus erit turmaeque Latinae
Tiburtique manus, ducis et tu concipe curam.'
sic ait, et paribus Messapum in proelia dictis 520
hortatur sociosque duces et pergit in hostem.
Est curuo anfractu ualles, accommoda fraudi
armorumque dolis, quam densis frondibus atrum
urget utrimque latus, tenuis quo semita ducit
angustaeque ferunt fauces aditusque maligni. 525
hanc super in speculis summoque in uertice montis
planities ignota iacet tutique receptus,
seu dextra laeuaque uelis occurrere pugnae
siue instare iugis et grandia uoluere saxa.
huc iuuenis nota fertur regione uiarum 530
arripuitque locum et siluis insedit iniquis.

500–31 MPR        503 turmis R        507 fixis M¹c        510 superat M¹        519
Tiburnique M¹P¹bfdhr, Seru. (cf. A. 7.671)        524 quo et qua Seru.        526 in (1°)]
e (A. 4.586 al.) Pf: om. R        uersum ante u. 525 ceu        527 receptus M¹Pω: recessus
M²P, 'male quidam' ap. Seru.

Velocem interea superis in sedibus Opim,
unam ex uirginibus sociis sacraque caterua,
compellabat et has tristis Latonia uoces
ore dabat: 'graditur bellum ad crudele Camilla,     535
o uirgo, et nostris nequiquam cingitur armis,
cara mihi ante alias. neque enim nouus iste Dianae
uenit amor subitaque animum dulcedine mouit.
pulsus ob inuidiam regno uirisque superbas
Priuerno antiqua Metabus cum excederet urbe,     540
infantem fugiens media inter proelia belli
sustulit exsilio comitem, matrisque uocauit
nomine Casmillae mutata parte Camillam.
ipse sinu prae se portans iuga longa petebat
solorum nemorum: tela undique saeua premebant     545
et circumfuso uolitabant milite Volsci.
ecce fugae medio summis Amasenus abundans
spumabat ripis, tantus se nubibus imber
ruperat. ille innare parans infantis amore
tardatur caroque oneri timet. omnia secum     550
uersanti subito uix haec sententia sedit:
telum immane manu ualida quod forte gerebat
bellator, solidum nodis et robore cocto,
huic natam libro et siluestri subere clausam
implicat atque habilem mediae circumligat hastae;     555
quam dextra ingenti librans ita ad aethera fatur:
'alma, tibi hanc, nemorum cultrix, Latonia uirgo,
ipse pater famulam uoueo; tua prima per auras
tela tenens supplex hostem fugit. accipe, testor,
diua tuam, quae nunc dubiis committitur auris.'     560
dixit, et adducto contortum hastile lacerto
immittit: sonuere undae, rapidum super amnem
infelix fugit in iaculo stridente Camilla.
at Metabus magna propius iam urgente caterua

532–64 MPR     533 sacris sociaque Re     534 tristi R     538 mouet euv
552 ferebat M²     554 huc R¹

dat sese fluuio, atque hastam cum uirgine uictor 565
gramineo, donum Triuiae, de caespite uellit.

Non illum tectis ullae, non moenibus urbes
accepere (neque ipse manus feritate dedisset),
pastorum et solis exegit montibus aeuum.
hic natam in dumis interque horrentia lustra 570
armentalis equae mammis et lacte ferino
nutribat teneris immulgens ubera labris.
utque pedum primis infans uestigia plantis
institerat, iaculo palmas armauit acuto
spiculaque ex umero paruae suspendit et arcum. 575
pro crinali auro, pro longae tegmine pallae
tigridis exuuiae per dorsum a uertice pendent.
tela manu iam tum tenera puerilia torsit
et fundam tereti circum caput egit habena
Strymoniamque gruem aut album deiecit olorem. 580
multae illam frustra Tyrrhena per oppida matres
optauere nurum; sola contenta Diana
aeternum telorum et uirginitatis amorem
intemerata colit. uellem haud correpta fuisset
militia tali conata lacessere Teucros: 585
cara mihi comitumque foret nunc una mearum.
uerum age, quandoquidem fatis urgetur acerbis,
labere, nympha, polo finisque inuise Latinos,
tristis ubi infausto committitur omine pugna.
haec cape et ultricem pharetra deprome sagittam: 590
hac, quicumque sacrum uiolarit uulnere corpus,
Tros Italusque, mihi pariter det sanguine poenas.
post ego nube caua miserandae corpus et arma
inspoliata feram tumulo patriaeque reponam.'
dixit, at illa leuis caeli delapsa per auras 595
insonuit nigro circumdata turbine corpus.

565–96 MPR    566 tollit P (G. 4.273)    574 armauit] onerauit (A. 10.868)
b, Seru.    592 Italusue (cf. A. 1.574, 10.108) bcfhr, Seru.; u. om. v    595 delapsa
Mfr: demissa (A. 10.73, 12.635) PRω, Tib.: dimissa bd

At manus interea muris Troiana propinquat,
Etruscique duces equitumque exercitus omnis
compositi numero in turmas. fremit aequore toto
insultans sonipes et pressis pugnat habenis                    600
huc conuersus et huc; tum late ferreus hastis
horret ager campique armis sublimibus ardent.
nec non Messapus contra celeresque Latini
et cum fratre Coras et uirginis ala Camillae
aduersi campo apparent, hastasque reductis              605
protendunt longe dextris et spicula uibrant,
aduentusque uirum fremitusque ardescit equorum.
iamque intra iactum teli progressus uterque
substiterat: subito erumpunt clamore furentisque
exhortantur equos, fundunt simul undique tela          610
crebra niuis ritu, caelumque obtexitur umbra.
continuo aduersis Tyrrhenus et acer Aconteus
conixi incurrunt hastis primique ruinam
dant sonitu ingenti perfractaque quadripedantum
pectora pectoribus rumpunt; excussus Aconteus        615
fulminis in morem aut tormento ponderis acti
praecipitat longe et uitam dispergit in auras.
Extemplo turbatae acies, uersique Latini
reiciunt parmas et equos ad moenia uertunt;
Troes agunt, princeps turmas inducit Asilas.              620
iamque propinquabant portis rursusque Latini
clamorem tollunt et mollia colla reflectunt;
hi fugiunt penitusque datis referuntur habenis.
qualis ubi alterno procurrens gurgite pontus
nunc ruit ad terram scopulosque superiacit unda    625

597–625 *MPR*      598 Etrurique *P¹dr*, 'quidam' *ap. DSeru.* (-iique *f*)      601
conuersus *MP*: obuersus *Rω*, *Tib.*      602 armis] hastis *P*      605 reductas
*M¹*      606 praetendunt *M¹*      609 substiterat *PM²ω*(-rant *bdr*): -uerant *R*:
constiterant *M¹*      612 aduersis *P¹ω*: aduersi *MP²R*      613 ruina *P²*      614
sonitu *Rω*: sonitum *MPu*  ingenti *MRω*: ingentem *P*      616 actus *P²*      624
procurrens *MP²b*: procumbens (*G*. 3.240) *P¹Rω*      625 terras *M*  suberigit (*cf.
Sil. Ital.* 15.155) *R*  unda *MPRbfhr*: undam *ω*, *Seru.*

spumeus extremamque sinu perfundit harenam,
nunc rapidus retro atque aestu reuoluta resorbens
saxa fugit litusque uado labente relinquit:
bis Tusci Rutulos egere ad moenia uersos,
bis reiecti armis respectant terga tegentes.                    630
tertia sed postquam congressi in proelia totas
implicuere inter se acies legitque uirum uir,
tum uero et gemitus morientum et sanguine in alto
armaque corporaque et permixti caede uirorum
semianimes uoluuntur equi, pugna aspera surgit.                 635
Orsilochus Remuli, quando ipsum horrebat adire,
hastam intorsit equo ferrumque sub aure reliquit;
quo sonipes ictu furit arduus altaque iactat
uulneris impatiens arrecto pectore crura,
uoluitur ille excussus humi. Catillus Iollan                    640
ingentemque animis, ingentem corpore et armis
deicit Herminium, nudo cui uertice fulua
caesaries nudique umeri nec uulnera terrent,
tantus in arma patet. latos huic hasta per armos
acta tremit duplicatque uirum transfixa dolore.                 645
funditur ater ubique cruor; dant funera ferro
certantes pulchramque petunt per uulnera mortem.
    At medias inter caedes exsultat Amazon
unum exserta latus pugnae, pharetrata Camilla,
et nunc lenta manu spargens hastilia denset,                    650
nunc ualidam dextra rapit indefessa bipennem;
aureus ex umero sonat arcus et arma Dianae.
illa etiam, si quando in tergum pulsa recessit,
spicula conuerso fugientia derigit arcu.
at circum lectae comites, Larinaque uirgo                       655

626–44 MPR; 645–55 MγR    637 relinquit aeruv    638 ferit M¹R    644
tantum R    645 premit γb    650 denset M²bd, DSeru.: densat M¹γRω,
Tib.    652 umeris Re, Tib.    653 in tergum si quando b, Tib.    654 fulgen-
tia Re    derigit MγR (degerit b, adegerit d): dirigit ω    655 et] et γb

Tullaque et aeratam quatiens Tarpeia securim,
Italides, quas ipsa decus sibi dia Camilla
delegit pacisque bonas bellique ministras:
quales Threiciae cum flumina Thermodontis
pulsant et pictis bellantur Amazones armis,                    660
seu circum Hippolyten seu cum se Martia curru
Penthesilea refert, magnoque ululante tumultu
feminea exsultant lunatis agmina peltis.

Quem telo primum, quem postremum, aspera uirgo,
deicis? aut quot humi morientia corpora fundis?              665
Eunaeum Clytio primum patre, cuius apertum
aduersi longa transuerberat abiete pectus.
sanguinis ille uomens riuos cadit atque cruentam
mandit humum moriensque suo se in uulnere uersat.
tum Lirim Pagasumque super, quorum alter habenas            670
suffuso reuolutus equo dum colligit, alter
dum subit ac dextram labenti tendit inermem,
praecipites pariterque ruunt. his addit Amastrum
Hippotaden, sequiturque incumbens eminus hasta
Tereaque Harpalycumque et Demophoonta Chromimque;           675
quotque emissa manu contorsit spicula uirgo,
tot Phrygii cecidere uiri. procul Ornytus armis
ignotis et equo uenator Iapyge fertur,
cui pellis latos umeros erepta iuuenco
pugnatori operit, caput ingens oris hiatus                   680
et malae texere lupi cum dentibus albis,
agrestisque manus armat sparus; ipse cateruis
uertitur in mediis et toto uertice supra, est.
hunc illa exceptum (neque enim labor) agmine uerso
traicit et super haec inimico pectore fatur:                685
'siluis te, Tyrrhene, feras agitare putasti?
aduenit qui uestra dies muliebribus armis

656–87 MγR     656 securem γ, Prisc. 7.53     657 dia M²γdv, Gramm., Seru.:
diua M¹ω: dura Rc?     658     bonas Myr: bonae Rω, Seru.     659 Thermodontis Mbf, Seru.: -doontis γRω     671 suffuso M²γRω, Seru., Tib.: sufosso M¹br,
'alii' ap. Seru.     672 inermem MRr: inertem γω     674 sequitur quem ceuv

uerba redargueret. nomen tamen haud leue patrum
manibus hoc referes, telo cecidisse Camillae.'
    Protinus Orsilochum et Buten, duo maxima Teucrum    690
corpora, sed Buten auersum cuspide fixit
loricam galeamque inter, qua colla sedentis
lucent et laeuo dependet parma lacerto;
Orsilochum fugiens magnumque agitata per orbem
eludit gyro interior sequiturque sequentem;    695
tum ualidam perque arma uiro perque ossa securim
altior exsurgens oranti et multa precanti
congeminat; uulnus calido rigat ora cerebro.
incidit huic subitoque aspectu territus haesit
Appenninicolae bellator filius Auni,    700
haud Ligurum extremus, dum fallere fata sinebant.
isque ubi se nullo iam cursu euadere pugnae
posse neque instantem reginam auertere cernit,
consilio uersare dolos ingressus et astu
incipit haec: 'quid tam egregium, si femina forti    705
fidis equo? dimitte fugam et te comminus aequo
mecum crede solo pugnaeque accinge pedestri:
iam nosces uentosa ferat cui gloria fraudem.'
dixit, at illa furens acrique accensa dolore
tradit equum comiti paribusque resistit in armis    710
ense pedes nudo puraque interrita parma.
at iuuenis uicisse dolo ratus auolat ipse
(haud mora), conuersisque fugax aufertur habenis
quadripedemque citum ferrata calce fatigat.
'uane Ligus frustraque animis elate superbis,    715
nequiquam patrias temptasti lubricus artis,
nec fraus te incolumem fallaci perferet Auno.'
haec fatur uirgo, et pernicibus ignea plantis
transit equum cursu frenisque aduersa prehensis
congreditur poenasque inimico ex sanguine sumit:    720

688–720 *MPR*    688 redarguerit *Prisc.* 10.10    691 aduersum ω (*praeter fr*)    707 pugnaque *bd*    708 fraudem $M^1P^1R$, '*uera et antiqua lectio*' iudice *Seru.*: laudem $M^2P^2$ω, *Tib.*    720 ex (*A.* 12.949)] a ω (*praeter bfr*)

quam facile accipiter saxo sacer ales ab alto
consequitur pennis sublimem in nube columbam
comprensamque tenet pedibusque euiscerat uncis;
tum cruor et uulsae labuntur ab aethere plumae.

At non haec nullis hominum sator atque deorum                    725
obseruans oculis summo sedet altus Olympo.
Tyrrhenum genitor Tarchonem in proelia saeua
suscitat et stimulis haud mollibus inicit iras.
ergo inter caedes cedentiaque agmina Tarchon
fertur equo uariisque instigat uocibus alas                      730
nomine quemque uocans, reficitque in proelia pulsos.
'quis metus, o numquam dolituri, o semper inertes
Tyrrheni, quae tanta animis ignauia uenit?
femina palantis agit atque haec agmina uertit?
quo ferrum quidue haec gerimus tela inrita dextris?              735
at non in Venerem segnes nocturnaque bella,
aut ubi curua choros indixit tibia Bacchi,
exspectate dapes et plenae pocula mensae
(hic amor, hoc studium) dum sacra secundus haruspex
nuntiet ac lucos uocet hostia pinguis in altos!'                740
haec effatus equum in medios moriturus et ipse
concitat, et Venulo aduersum se turbidus infert
dereptumque ab equo dextra complectitur hostem
et gremium ante suum multa ui concitus aufert.
tollitur in caelum clamor cunctique Latini                       745
conuertere oculos. uolat igneus aequore Tarchon
arma uirumque ferens; tum summa ipsius ab hasta
defringit ferrum et partis rimatur apertas,
qua uulnus letale ferat; contra ille repugnans
sustinet a iugulo dextram et uim uiribus exit.                   750
utque uolans alte raptum cum fulua draconem
fert aquila implicuitque pedes atque unguibus haesit,
saucius at serpens sinuosa uolumina uersat

721–36 MPR; 737–53 MγR        728 inicit Rω: incitat (cf. A. 10.263) MPbfr:
incutit N. Heinsius        735 geritis cehruv, Tib.        738 mensae] dextrae γ        741
et ipse] in hostis (A. 9.554) γ        742 infert Mω: offert γR, Tib.

arrectisque horret squamis et sibilat ore
arduus insurgens, illa haud minus urget obunco 755
luctantem rostro, simul aethera uerberat alis:
haud aliter praedam Tiburtum ex agmine Tarchon
portat ouans. ducis exemplum euentumque secuti
Maeonidae incurrunt. tum fatis debitus Arruns
uelocem iaculo et multa prior arte Camillam 760
circuit, et quae sit fortuna facillima temptat.
qua se cumque furens medio tulit agmine uirgo,
hac Arruns subit et tacitus uestigia lustrat;
qua uictrix redit illa pedemque ex hoste reportat,
hac iuuenis furtim celeris detorquet habenas. 765
hos aditus iamque hos aditus omnemque pererrat
undique circuitum et certam quatit improbus hastam.
Forte sacer Cybelo Chloreus olimque sacerdos
insignis longe Phrygiis fulgebat in armis
spumantemque agitabat equum, quem pellis aënis 770
in plumam squamis auro conserta tegebat.
ipse peregrina ferrugine clarus et ostro
spicula torquebat Lycio Gortynia cornu;
aureus ex umeris erat arcus et aurea uati
cassida; tum croceam chlamydemque sinusque crepantis 775
carbaseos fuluo in nodum collegerat auro
pictus acu tunicas et barbara tegmina crurum.
hunc uirgo, siue ut templis praefigeret arma
Troia, captiuo siue ut se ferret in auro
uenatrix, unum ex omni certamine pugnae 780
caeca sequebatur totumque incauta per agmen
femineo praedae et spoliorum ardebat amore,
telum ex insidiis cum tandem tempore capto
concitat et superos Arruns sic uoce precatur:

754–756 MγR; 757–82 Mγa; 783–4 MPa      755 obunco Mγf (-cto c): adunco
Rruv: abunco bdeh (cf. A. 6.597)      759 fatis tum aev, f. tantum u      766
iamque] atque γ      768 Cybelo Maω, Seru., Tib.: Cybele γ: Cybelae Macrob.
5.1.12 (cf. A. 3.111)      774 umero (u. 652) γ      erat] sonat γcdfh      781 incensa
(A. 4.300) dh      784 conicit (A. 9.411, 10.646) cdfh

'summe deum, sancti custos Soractis Apollo,                    785
quem primi colimus, cui pineus ardor aceruo
pascitur, et medium freti pietate per ignem
cultores multa premimus uestigia pruna,
da, pater, hoc nostris aboleri dedecus armis,
omnipotens. non exuuias pulsaeue tropaeum                      790
uirginis aut spolia ulla peto, mihi cetera laudem
facta ferent; haec dira meo dum uulnere pestis
pulsa cadat, patrias remeabo inglorius urbes.'
    Audiit et uoti Phoebus succedere partem
mente dedit, partem uolucris dispersit in auras:              795
sterneret ut subita turbatam morte Camillam
adnuit oranti; reducem ut patria alta uideret
non dedit, inque Notos uocem uertere procellae.
ergo ut missa manu sonitum dedit hasta per auras,
conuertere animos acris oculosque tulere                      800
cuncti ad reginam Volsci. nihil ipsa nec aurae
nec sonitus memor aut uenientis ab aethere teli,
hasta sub exsertam donec perlata papillam
haesit uirgineumque alte bibit acta cruorem.
concurrunt trepidae comites dominamque ruentem                805
suscipiunt. fugit ante omnis exterritus Arruns
laetitia mixtoque metu, nec iam amplius hastae
credere nec telis occurrere uirginis audet.
ac uelut ille, prius quam tela inimica sequantur,
continuo in montis sese auius abdidit altos                   810
occiso pastore lupus magnoue iuuenco,
conscius audacis facti, caudamque remulcens
subiecit pauitantem utero siluasque petiuit:
haud secus ex oculis se turbidus abstulit Arruns
contentusque fuga mediis se immiscuit armis.                  815

785–92 *MPa*; 793–815 *MPR*    786 primis *P*[1]    789 aboleri *M²Pbdhr*:
abolere *M¹aω*    792 ferant *du*    794 uotis *Macrob.* 5.3.7    partem succ.
Phoebus *b*    799 ut] ubi *M*¹    801 neque *cdfh*    auras (*cf. u.* 795, 799) *d*,
'antiqua lectio' *Seru.*, *ut sit genetiuus singularis*

illa manu moriens telum trahit, ossa sed inter
ferreus ad costas alto stat uulnere mucro.
labitur exsanguis, labuntur frigida leto
lumina, purpureus quondam color ora reliquit.
tum sic exspirans Accam ex aequalibus unam          820
adloquitur, fida ante alias quae sola Camillae
quicum partiri curas, atque haec ita fatur:
'hactenus, Acca soror, potui: nunc uulnus acerbum
conficit, et tenebris nigrescunt omnia circum.
effuge et haec Turno mandata nouissima perfer:     825
succedat pugnae Troianosque arceat urbe.
iamque uale.' simul his dictis linquebat habenas
ad terram non sponte fluens. tum frigida toto
paulatim exsoluit se corpore, lentaque colla
et captum leto posuit caput, arma relinquens,      830
uitaque cum gemitu fugit indignata sub umbras.
tum uero immensus surgens ferit aurea clamor
sidera: deiecta crudescit pugna Camilla;
incurrunt densi simul omnis copia Teucrum
Tyrrhenique duces Euandrique Arcades alae.         835
    At Triuiae custos iamdudum in montibus Opis
alta sedet summis spectatque interrita pugnas.
utque procul medio iuuenum in clamore furentum
prospexit tristi mulcatam morte Camillam,
ingemuitque deditque has imo pectore uoces:        840
'heu nimium, uirgo, nimium crudele luisti
supplicium Teucros conata lacessere bello!
nec tibi desertae in dumis coluisse Dianam
profuit aut nostras umero gessisse pharetras.

816–44 *MPR*    818 leto] telo *'alii' ap. Seru.*    819 relinquit *c*    821 fida
*M¹Rω*: fidam *M²P* (fidem *b*)    822 quicum *M Rbd*: quacum *Pω*    826 urbe
*MP²ω*, *Tib.*: urbi (*cf. E.* 7.47) *P¹R*    830 relinquens *M²P²ω*: relinquit *M¹*:
reliquit *P¹R*: relinquunt *'alii'* (*inter quos Probus*) *ap. DSeru.*, *Tib.*    834 concurrunt *Re*    835 Tyrrhenumque *M* (*cf. u* 171)    838 iuuenem medio *P¹*:
medio iuuenem *b*   furentem *M²*(-te *M¹*)*b*, *interpr. Tib.*    839 mulcatam
*MPRbdr*, *DSeru.*: multatam *fortasse recte ω*    844 pharetras *PRω*: sagittas *Mchr*

non tamen indecorem tua te regina reliquit                           845
extrema iam in morte, neque hoc sine nomine letum
per gentis erit aut famam patieris inultae.
nam quicumque tuum uiolauit uulnere corpus
morte luet merita.' fuit ingens monte sub alto
regis Dercenni terreno ex aggere bustum                              850
antiqui Laurentis opacaque ilice tectum;
hic dea se primum rapido pulcherrima nisu
sistit et Arruntem tumulo speculatur ab alto.
ut uidit fulgentem armis ac uana tumentem,
'cur' inquit 'diuersus abis? huc derige gressum,                     855
huc periture ueni, capias ut digna Camillae
praemia. tune etiam telis moriere Dianae?'
dixit, et aurata uolucrem Threissa sagittam
deprompsit pharetra cornuque infensa tetendit
et duxit longe, donec curuata coirent                                860
inter se capita et manibus iam tangeret aequis,
laeua aciem ferri, dextra neruoque papillam.
extemplo teli stridorem aurasque sonantis
audiit una Arruns haesitque in corpore ferrum.
illum exspirantem socii atque extrema gementem                       865
obliti ignoto camporum in puluere linquunt;
Opis ad aetherium pennis aufertur Olympum.

Prima fugit domina amissa leuis ala Camillae,
turbati fugiunt Rutuli, fugit acer Atinas,
disiectique duces desolatique manipli                                870
tuta petunt et equis auersi ad moenia tendunt.
nec quisquam instantis Teucros letumque ferentis
sustentare ualet telis aut sistere contra,
sed laxos referunt umeris languentibus arcus,
quadripedumque putrem cursu quatit ungula campum.                    875

845–57 MPR; 858–75 FMPR      845 reliquit MPf: relinquet Pω: relinquit r,
Tib.      846 numine efh      852 dea] ea M¹      854 laetantem animis M¹
856 Camilla R      861 tenderet bd      870 disiectique] defectique M¹      871
equos P      aduersi cev      875 quadripedoque F¹Rr, Tib. (cf. A. 8.596)

uoluitur ad muros caligine turbidus atra
puluis, et e speculis percussae pectora matres
femineum clamorem ad caeli sidera tollunt.
qui cursu portas primi inrupere patentis,
hos inimica super mixto premit agmine turba,          880
nec miseram effugiunt mortem, sed limine in ipso,
moenibus in patriis atque inter tuta domorum
confixi exspirant animas. pars claudere portas,
nec sociis aperire uiam nec moenibus audent
accipere orantis, oriturque miserrima caedes          885
defendentum armis aditus inque arma ruentum,
exclusi ante oculos lacrimantumque ora parentum
pars in praecipitis fossas urgente ruina
uoluitur, immissis pars caeca et concita frenis
arietat in portas et duros obice postis.          890
ipsae de muris summo certamine matres
(monstrat amor uerus patriae, ut uidere Camillam)
tela manu trepidae iaciunt ac robore duro
stipitibus ferrum sudibusque imitantur obustis
praecipites, primaeque mori pro moenibus ardent.          895
    Interea Turnum in siluis saeuissimus implet
nuntius et iuueni ingentem fert Acca tumultum:
deletas Volscorum acies, cecidisse Camillam,
ingruere infensos hostis et Marte secundo
omnia corripuisse, metum iam ad moenia ferri.          900
ille furens (et saeua Iouis sic numina poscunt)
deserit obsessos collis, nemora aspera linquit.
uix e conspectu exierat campumque tenebat,
cum pater Aeneas saltus ingressus apertos
exsuperatque iugum siluaque euadit opaca.          905
sic ambo ad muros rapidi totoque feruntur
agmine nec longis inter se passibus absunt;

876–95 FMPR; 896–907 MPR          877 e om. F¹M¹br   speculis] muris cdf
882 inter FPbcdfhr: intra MReuv          892 uersus R          895 audent M²ω (praeter
r), Seru.          901 poscunt (A. 8.512)] pellunt R          903 camposque M¹

ac simul Aeneas fumantis puluere campos
prospexit longe Laurentiaque agmina uidit,
et saeuum Aenean agnouit Turnus in armis     910
aduentumque pedum flatusque audiuit equorum.
continuoque ineant pugnas et proelia temptent,
ni roseus fessos iam gurgite Phoebus Hibero
tingat equos noctemque die labente reducat.
considunt castris ante urbem et moenia uallant.     915

908–15 *MPR*     908 ac simul] tum pater (*u.* 904) *PReuv*     909 conspexit *b*
910 agnouit] conspexit *P*     911 aduentusque *Mr, Tib.* (*cf. u.* 607)    flatumque
*Rev*     912 ineunt *M¹b*    temptant *c*

# COMMENTARY

## 1–28 Prologue

Aeneas dedicates the armour of Mezentius, killed by him at the end of book x (see Introd. 7–10), to Mars the god of war, and orders funeral rites for Pallas and the rest of those slain in the fighting narrated in book x.

**1** This is the only book of the *Aeneid* to start with a temporal formula. It marks the beginning of a new day after the momentous one which saw the deaths of Pallas, Lausus and Mezentius in book x. This new day ends at 181, after which two further days are occupied with the burial and burning of the dead. A third day begins at 209, ending at the end of the book with another temporal formula. The present v. = 4.129, where it introduces the hunting-party at Carthage: there is another ref. to Dido at 74–5. On the two passages see further Newman, *CET* 164–5.

**interea:** introducing a narrative transition; cf. 532, 10.1.

**2 quamquam et:** for this type of elision or aphaeresis of a monosyllable at the beginning of the 3rd foot, much favoured by V., see Gransden on 8.10; Soubiran 181–3, 286, 526–8; Hellegouarc'h 135–50. *et* is picked up by *-que* in the following v.

**3 praecipitant curae** 'his anxieties urge him on': the constr. with the infin. is imitated by Statius, *Theb.* 1.679 *sed si praecipitant miserum cognoscere curae.*

**funere:** most edd. and translators follow Servius in referring this to the death of Pallas, though it could be more general. Conington says that the idea of death in general troubling Aen. would be out of keeping with Virgilian feeling: a strange comment.

**4 uota deum** 'vows to the gods': a kind of possessive gen.; since the vows are the gods' due, they belong to them.

**uota ... uictor soluebat:** cf. 8.61–2 *uictor honorem | persolues* (another dawn-ritual).

**Eoo** 'dawn-light'. *Eous* is an adj. used as a noun by V. here and at 3.588 *dies primo surgebat Eoo*, *Georg.* 1.288 *terras inrorat Eous.*

**5–11** As Conington remarks, this is a *locus classicus* for the construction of a war-trophy, a tree-trunk decked with the arms of a dead foe.

69

It is an instance of Virgilian 'anachronism' or rather 'synchronism': a practice current in the army in the poet's own time is introduced into the primitive Italy of Aeneas' time. The passage is full of epic grandeur, secured by such devices as the apostrophe to Mars at 7, the enjambment at 7–8, alliteration (*t, p, s*), and assonance (*cristas, sinistrae*).

**9 trunca** 'broken'; the word also suggests the lopped trunk. Cf. Suet. *Cal.* 45 *truncatis arboribus et in modum tropaeorum adornatis.*

**bis sex:** such round numbers need not be taken literally in poetry.

**thoraca:** Greek accus.: 'his breastplate attacked and penetrated . . .'

**10–11 sinistrae:** sc. *parti.*

**collo** continues the identification of the tree-trunk with the dead hero of whom it is a symbol.

**ex aere** 'made of bronze': also at 5.266, and cf. 850.

**eburnum:** this may refer to the scabbard (cf. 9.305) or perhaps the handle.

**12 eum:** the pronoun *is* is rare in Latin poetry. *eum* occurs six times in the *Aen.*: see Austin on 4.479, where both *eum* and *eo* occur.

**14 maxima ... uiri:** cf. *Il.* 22.393, where Achilles says, after killing Hector, ἠράμεθα μέγα κῦδος, 'we have won great glory'. *est* is to be understood: the ellipse is frequent in Latin, cf. 17.

**15 quod superest** 'as regards what remains (to be done)': cf. 9.157.

**de rege superbo** is to be taken both with *spolia* and with *primitiae* in the following line. For the word-order cf. 19–21n. *de* is elliptical as in dedicatory inscriptions, cf. 3.288 *Aeneas haec de Danais uictoribus arma.* Some word like *erepta* may be understood in the present passage.

**16 manibusque ... est** 'by my hands, *this* is Mezentius' (i.e. this is what he has become). Aeneas speaks here in the self-vaunting tone of the traditional epic hero. *manibus* is abl. of agent, as at 2.192; *hic* is emphatically deictic, reinforcing *haec* above, as Page noted; Servius compares 9.481 *hunc ego te, Euryale, aspicio?* It should not be translated 'here' as Williams does.

**18** No comma is required after *parate*; it is far more in V.'s manner to offer a pair of balanced cola, the second amplifying the first (see further the next n.). For *animis = animose*, and for the whole constr., cf. 491.

**19–21** 'Lest, taken unawares, any delay should hold us back or feebleness of purpose slow us down in fear, when once the gods have given us their approval to strike camp and lead our young men forth from base.' A characteristically extended Virgilian construction, comprising two pairs of parallel cola (cf. 18 above), of which one pair (introduced by *ubi primum*) is 'interlaced' with the other (introduced by *ne qua*). The sense of the whole cannot be grasped until the reading of the three lines is completed; the structure is circular, not linear (cf. 15): words distant from each other must be connected by the reader; here *mora* cannot be taken with the adjacent *ignaros* until line 21, when the verb which links the two words appears. This is a characteristic of all Latin syntax which Virgil exploits with particular skill and flexibility. See further J. P. Postgate, 'Flaws in Classical research', *P.B.A.* 3 (1909) 7–9.

**19 ignaros** 'ignorant' (because unprepared).

**uellere signa** (cf. *Georg.* 4.108, Livy 3.50.11) is the technical term for going into battle; when the army was encamped behind its own lines the standards were fixed in the ground, and were pulled out before moving into action. Here the sense is reinforced by the variant *pubemque educere castra* which forms the second 'limb' of the pair of cola.

**20 adnuerint:** sc. *nobis*; here with the infin. (cf. 10.8 *abnueram ... concurrere*), at 796 with *ut* + subj.

**21 impediat** is governed by *mora* at 19: another good ex. of V.'s fondness for a binary structure: *segnisue ... tardet* balances and reinforces *mora ... impediat*.

**22 socios inhumataque corpora** 'the unburied bodies of our comrades' (hendiadys): cf. 64.

**23 mandemus** 'let us commit to earth', as in the Christian burial-service.

**qui ... imo est:** cf. *Il.* 16.457 τὸ γάρ γέρας ἐστὶ θανόντων, 'for this is the honour due to the dead'. The relative pronoun *qui* agrees with the predicate (*honos*); it does not take its gender from the antecedent clause.

**24–5** 'Who have won this as our fatherland with their blood': *patriam* is emphatically predicative. Aeneas rises to this peroration in language which is eloquently alliterative.

**26 maestamque:** on this key-word, which occurs 11 times in book XI, 14 times in books I–VIII and 9 times in books IX, X and XII, see further Introd. 28.

**27 non uirtutis egentem:** litotes, or affirmation by negation of the contrary. A common figure: cf. 8.299 *non . . . rationis egentem*, and phrases with *haud* at, e.g., 64, 106.

**28** ´ = 6.429 (cf. also 6.272, where *nox abstulit atra* occurs in the description of the entrance to the underworld).

**acerbo** 'bitter', 'cruel': for the metaphorical use cf. 587 *fatis . . . acerbis.*

### 29–99 Pallas' funeral cortège

**30 positum** 'laid out'. Acoetes, Evander's aged squire, is mentioned only here and at 85: see 32–3 n.

**31 Parrhasio Euandro:** the hiatus and spondee in the 5th foot produce a rhythm common in Homer but rare in Latin. The effect occurs five times in the *Aen.*, always with proper names: cf. 1.617, 3.74, 7.631 (see Fordyce's n. on spondaic hexameters in general), 9.647.

**Parrhasio:** the epithet is probably conventional, like *Dardanius Aeneas*, rather than predicative, 'in his Arcadian days' (Conington).

**32–3 sed non . . . alumno** 'but he was not marching then with such happy auspices as companion to his dear protégé' (i.e. as he did when he was Evander's squire and when E. gave him wardship over Pallas). The pathos and the bold, dramatic compression of these words are characteristic of V. For Acoetes' role as *armiger* cf. 9.648 where Butes, formerly *armiger* to Anchises, is chosen by Aeneas to look after Ascanius.

**aeque:** the ending of a line with an 'indifferent' or colourless word (preposition, intensifier, adverb, etc.) with enjambment is characteristic of V.'s later style: cf. 51, 57, 164, 170, 201, 204, 205, 282, 374, 409, 429, 471, 484, 499, 504, 509, 550, 671, 683, 712, 741, 794, 816, 824, 873. Cf. Introd. 31.

**34 famulumque:** the original form of the gen. pl. second declension survived, as old forms tend to do, in a number of formal and official expressions and as an archaism in the epic style: see Fordyce on 7.189. It is common in Lucretius (*deum, diuum, uirum,* etc.).

**35 crinem . . . solutae:** the accus. with a passive participle is a favourite constr. of V.'s. The participle is often used in a 'middle' or reflexive sense with the part of the body affected, as here and at 480, 507, 596, 649, 877, or with the object put on, as at 487 (*indutus*, used in the middle sense from Plautus on), 777. Cf. Williams on 7.503.

**36 foribus sese intulit altis:** cf. 12.441 *portis sese extulit ingens.*

**37–8 tunsis ... pectoribus** 'with beating of breasts': perf. participle passive used here in its original sense, without reference to the past: cf. 8.407–8.

**38 immugit:** this word has not been found before V., who uses it twice, here and (of Etna) at 3.674. For a similar metaphor with *mugire* (the earth groaning) cf. 4.490, 6.256.

**39–41** The emotional effect of these lines is heightened by the alliterative patterns.

**39 caput ... et ora** 'the head and face of snow-white Pallas resting there'. *et* is epexegetic: the second phrase parallels, explains or paraphrases the first rather than adding to it (Hofmann–Szantyr 782–3). The usage is frequent: cf. 8.38 *solo Laurenti aruisque Latinis.*

**fultum** 'propped up'.

**40 lēuique** 'smooth', 'soft'; also used of a woman, 7.349. V. wants to stress P.'s adolescent beauty.

**42–58** On this speech, one of the focal points of the entire poem, see Introd. 26; Gransden, *VI* 161–4.

**42 miserande puer:** also used of Lausus, 10.825, and Marcellus, 6.882. V. characteristically associates in the reader's mind examples of the same figure, the young man untimely dead (cf. Introd. 5). We may perhaps compare A. E. Housman:

> Here dead we lie because we did not choose
> To live, and shame the land from which we sprung.
> Life, to be sure, is nothing much to lose,
> But young men think it is, and we were young,
>
> (*More Poems* (1936) xxxvi).

**42–3 tene ... inuidit ... ne ... uideres** 'did Fortune grudge you to me, though she came smiling? You were not to see our kingdom established.' The subordinate clause, here with *ne*, expresses 'the thing grudged'. Cf. 269–70, where 'the thing grudged' is expressed with *ut*: two MSS read *ne* there also. The English constr. with 'lest' or 'that' after verbs of fearing exhibits a similar grammatical ambiguity but no ambiguity of meaning.

These vv. offer a marked alliteration of consonantal *u*, sustained to v. 44, together with assonance and word-play (*inuidit ... uideres*).

**45–52** This celebrated passage represents one of V.'s finest transformations of Homer. Verses 45–8 allude to Achilles' lament for Patroclus, *Il.* 18.324–7; 49–52 allude to Andromache at *Il.* 22.437–46, where she sets about preparing Hector's bath, unaware that he is already dead. V. has replaced the domestic detail with something deeply ritualistic and Roman: Aen. imagines Evander at prayer. For the structure of the passage cf. also 10.839–42, where Mezentius is about to face the death of his son Lausus: *multa super Lauso rogitat, multumque remittit | qui reuocent maestique ferant mandata parentis. | at Lausum socii exanimem super arma ferebant | flentes, ingentem atque ingenti uulnere uictum.*

**45 non haec:** this emphatic opening (cf. 152) echoes Catullus 64.139–40 *non haec quondam ... promissa dedisti.*

**47 mitteret in magnum imperium:** cf. 6.812 *missus in imperium magnum. imperium* can mean either 'command' or 'empire'. There is no need to rule out either meaning, as Henry and Conington do.

**49 multum:** adverbial ('much deceived').

**50 fors et uota facit** 'perhaps is even now making his vows' (prayers of promises to the gods for Pallas' safety). For this use of *fors et* cf. 2.139 with Austin's n., Nisbet and Hubbard on Hor. *C.* 1.28.31.

**51–2** For the structure of these lines cf. 865–6.

**nil ... debentem** 'owing nothing now to any of the gods above'; any debts Pallas still has to pay must now be paid to the gods of the underworld. *caelestibus* is emphatic: only the living have such obligations. For the sentiment cf. Soph. *Ajax* 589–90 οὐ κάτοισθ', ἐγὼ θεοῖς | ὡς οὐδὲν ἄρκειν εἴμ' ὀφειλέτης ἔτι, 'Do you not know that I no longer owe any service to the gods?'

**54** For the symmetry cf. 870, 8.263. This and the following half-line are spoken in bitter irony.

**55–7 at non ... pater** 'But then you will never see him in retreat, Evander, shamefully wounded, nor, as a father, pray for an accursed death while he lives safely on.' Evander's only consolation must lie in escaping the shame he might have had to endure if Pallas had behaved dishonourably in saving his skin. The sense of the passage is not in doubt, but the Latin is highly compressed and cannot easily be translated without considerable expansion.

**57 ei mihi:** cf. 2.274, 12.620; Ennius, *Ann.* 442 *ei mihi, qualis erat ...*

**59 defleuit:** of a formal lamentation; also at 6.220. See Kenney on Lucr. 3.907.

**61 qui ... comitentur** 'to accompany'; *qui = ut ii*: cf. 7.98, 8.10, 9.193, 10.518. See also 81n.

**62 intersintque** 'participate in': a prose word found only here in V.

**62–3 solacia ... ingentis** 'small consolation for a great sorrow', accus. in apposition to the previous sentence, which it extends and comments on: cf. 2.223 *triste ministerium*, 8.487 *tormenti genus*.

**64 haud segnes:** cf. 27n.

**cratis et molle feretrum** 'a soft bier of wicker-work' (hendiadys).

**65** Another good ex. of V.'s fondness for binary structure (cf. 18, 64, Introd. 29). On the arrangement of pairs of nouns and adjectives in V. see Norden Anh. iii.397. The bier is plaited with thin branches of oak saplings and arbute (the evergreen 'strawberry tree', *Arbutus unedo*, mentioned at *Ecl.* 3.82, on which see Coleman's n.).

**66–8** These three vv. are markedly Catullan: all have a word of three long syllables after the caesura, a rhythm common in Catullus' hexameters but used by V. sparingly.

**67 stramine:** *stramen* has not been found to occur before V., who uses it only here. Forms in *-men* were much favoured by Ovid, who has *stramen* several times.

**68–71** This celebrated simile should be compared with that at 9.435–7 (the death of Euryalus): *purpureus ueluti cum flos succisus aratro | languescit moriens, lassoue papauera collo | demisere caput pluuia cum forte grauantur.* The poppy is from Homer, *Il.* 8.306–8 (the head of Gorgythion lolls in death like the head of a poppy dropping under its own weight) but the present simile is profoundly un-Homeric. It is in fact a reworking of Catullus 62.39–47, a passage which V. evidently had much in mind (see also n. on 581):

> Vt flos in saeptis secretus nascitur hortis,
> ignotus pecori, nullo conuolsus aratro,
> quem mulcent aurae, format sol, educat imber;
> multi illum pueri, multae optauere puellae:
> idem cum tenui carptus defloruit ungui,
> nulli illum pueri, nullae optauere puellae:
> sic uirgo, dum intacta manet, dum cara suis est;
> cum castum amisit polluto corpore florem,
> nec pueris iucunda manet, nec cara puellis.

The erotic poignancy of V.'s transformation of Catullus' lines derives from its central motif, that of virginity lost, not to marriage, as it should be (Catullus 62 is a marriage-poem), but to death. Once the precious flower of virginity is plucked, an irreversible change occurs: in the case of Pallas or Euryalus, the ultimate transformation by the sterile bridegroom, death. The untimely deaths of these young men mean that they will now never achieve full manhood, marriage and children: the body of Pallas, its erotic beauty not yet faded, lies like a tableau before the reader. See further Introd. 11; Gransden, *VI* 114–19; Johnson 59–66; Newman, *CET* 165–6; D. West, 'Multiple correspondence similes in the *Aeneid*', *J.R.S.* 59 (1969) 47; and D. Gillis, *Eros and death in the Aeneid* (Rome 1983) 77–79, an interesting discussion in the course of which the following illuminating lines are quoted from Robert Lowell's poem 'Falling asleep over the Aeneid':

> Face of snow,
> You are the flower that country girls have caught,
> A wild bee-pillaged honeysuckle brought
> To the returning bridegroom – the design
> Has not yet left it, and the petals shine;
> The earth, its mother, has at last no help;
> It is itself.

**68 uirgineo ... pollice** 'a young girl's hand': *pollice* stands for *manu* (the figure called synecdoche) as does *ungui* in Catullus 62.43. The adj. is particularly poignant, for the reader will transfer it from the maiden who plucks the flower, to Pallas, the flower itself.

**69 languentis hyacinthi:** the final syllable of *languentis* is treated as 'long' before a Greek quadrisyllable beginning with a vowel or *h*. Cf. *Ecl.* 6.53 *fultus hyacintho*, *Aen.* 10.720 *profugus hymenaeos*. See also 614n.

**70** 'From which neither its radiance nor its beauty has yet departed'. Another instance of binary structure, the second half of the line a variation on the first. The pathos is emphasised by the alliteration of *fulgor ... forma*.

**72 -que ... -que:** an epic mannerism in imitation of the double τε of Homer and the Alexandrians. V. has it more than 150 times in the *Aen.*, usually with words parallel in form or function: cf. 92–3 *Teucrique ... Tyrrhenique*, 150 *lacrimansque gemensque*.

**73 laeta laborum** 'happy in the work': gen. of respect or sphere. Cf. 338 *largus opum*, 416 *fortunatus ... laborum*.

**75** Repeated from 4.262. The correspondence offers the reader a moment of disturbing irony. Pallas, like Dido, is a victim of A.'s relentless destiny.

**76 supremum ... honorem** 'as a last honour': in apposition to *unam*.

**76–7** Aen. chooses one of a pair of cloaks given him by Dido and uses it to shroud the corpse 'and cover those locks the fire will burn' (theme and variation). Many commentators follow Servius in assuming that Aen. used both cloaks, one for the body, one for the head, but V. does not say this. Cf. *Il.* 24.580–91, where two cloaks are also mentioned. Macleod assumes that both cloaks are put over the body of Hector, but Homer (like V.) does not actually say so.

**78 Laurentis:** V. uses this adj. generally to refer to Latinus' people and region: see Gransden on 8.1.

**81–4** 'He had also bound behind their backs the hands (of those) whom he intended to send to their death, being prepared to sprinkle the fire with their blood, and now he gave orders for the leaders themselves to carry the trophies adorned with the arms of the foe, and for the names of the enemy to be inscribed thereon.'

This *acte gratuit* shows Aen. to be no less capable of atavistic *furor* than Turnus, or than Homer's Achilles, who likewise selected twelve prisoners, bound their hands behind their backs and later sacrificed them on Patroclus' pyre (*Il.* 21.27, 23.175). There may also be a covert reference here to the human sacrifice reported as having been undertaken by Octavian in honour of Julius Caesar (Suet. *Aug.* 15).

**81 quos mitteret:** the subject is Aeneas, and *eorum* must be supplied as the antecedent to *quos*; *mitteret* is a final subj.

**82 inferias** 'as offerings'.

**84 inimicaque nomina:** Williams quotes an apposite passage from Tacitus, *Ann.* 2.18 *in modum tropaeorum arma subscriptis uictarum gentium nominibus imposuit.*

**87 sternitur et** 'as he throws himself down'. The actions described in this v. must be taken simultaneously not consecutively: see 19–21n.

**88** The bloody chariots are from Homer, *Il.* 11.534–5 (= 20.499–500).

**89 bellator equus:** cf. 10.891. Aethon is also the name of one of Hector's horses (*Il.* 8.185).

**90** For the weeping horse cf. Homer, *Il.* 17.426–7, where Achilles'

horses weep for Patroclus. The motif found its way into Roman lore:
Williams refers to Suet. *Jul.* 81 (Caesar's horses weep at the prospect of
his death) and Pliny, *N.H.* 8.157, where it is said that horses weep when
they lose their masters.

**91 cetera:** this refers to Pallas' baldric which Turnus took: see
10.500 *quo nunc Turnus ouat spolio gaudetque potitus.* Missing from the
funeral, it will reappear, worn by Turnus, at the final confrontation
between T. and Aen., 12.941–2.

**92 maesta phalanx** is explained by what follows: *-que, -que* and *et*
are all epexegetic.

**93 uersis ... armis** must be taken with all the contingents mentioned. Reversed arms were a feature of Roman military funerals: cf.
Tacitus, *Ann.* 3.2, on Germanicus' funeral (*uersi fasces*).

**94 praecesserat** 'had gone forward'. Aen., having accompanied
the cortège a short distance as a mark of respect, now makes his farewell
to Pallas and returns to camp.

**96–8** One of the shortest of Aen.'s speeches and one of the most
touching. The Homeric model is Achilles' farewell to Patroclus (*Il.*
23.179–83), but V. has removed any trace of revenge from his words.
The opening recalls Aen.'s farewell to Andromache, 3.493–4 (*nos alia
ex aliis in fata uocamur*), while the close echoes Catullus' farewell to his
brother, 101.10 (*in perpetuum ... aue atque uale*).

**97–8 salue ... uale** replaces the more usual formula (*h*)*aue atque uale.*

**97 aeternum** 'for ever': adverbial, for the more usual *in aeternum, in
perpetuum*; not found before V. (cf. 6.617 *sedet aeternumque sedebit*) and
Horace (*Ep.* 1.10.41 *seruiet aeternum, quia paruo nesciet uti.*).

**mihi:** dat. of agent.

## 100–224 The truce and the burning and burial of the dead

For the Homeric models see Introd. 12–13.

**100 oratores** 'ambassadors'.

**101** The olive branch, sacred to Pallas Athene, was carried as a sign
of peace, cf. 332, 7.153–4 *centum oratores augusta ad moenia regis* | *ire iubet,
ramis uelatos Palladis omnis.*

**ueniamque** 'favour', 'indulgence'.

**102–5** The ambassadors' petition is given in *oratio obliqua*: cf. 8.10–
17, and for the form of such diplomatic proposals see Highet 55–6.

The subjunctives *redderet . . . sineret . . . parceret* are indirect imperatives dependent on *rogantes*.

**102 per . . . iacebant:** this descriptive clause is in the indicative because it is not to be regarded as part of the ambassadors' request, but as an explanatory gloss on *corpora* in the 'voice' of the epic narrator.

**104** This line is part of the ambassadors' petition, but the construction has been changed to the accus. and infin. of oblique narration: the verb *esse* must be supplied.

**aethere cassis** 'those bereft of the light', i.e. the dead. Cf. 2.85 *cassum lumine*, with Austin's n., and for *aether* = 'the light of life', 'the upper world' cf. 6.436 *aethere in alto*, 1.546–7 *aura aetheria*. V. has characteristically transformed a Lucretian scientific formula *cassum lumine*, 'devoid of light', into a metaphor full of the pathos of mortality.

**105** The ambassadors remind Aen. of Latinus' pledge at their first meeting, 7.264 *si iungi hospitio properat sociusque uocari*.

**106 bonus** for the more usual *pius*: also at 5.770.

**haud aspernanda** 'not to be refused': cf. 27n.

**107 prosequitur** 'sends on their way': cf. 6.476 *prosequitur lacrimis*, 12.72–3 *ne me lacrimis neue omine tanto prosequere*. Here, by a boldly extended figure, Aen. is said to 'see off' the envoys *uenia*, 'with their request granted'.

**108–119** The last of the four speeches of Aen. in book XI. It begins with a sorrowful and characteristic question which resembles the words of Diomedes reported by Venulus at 253–4.

**108–111** A powerful statement of Aen.'s and the implied author's hatred of war, built on the antitheses *bello/pacem* and *Martis sorte peremptis/uiuis*.

**109 qui nos fugiatis amicos** 'that you should shun us who are your friends'. The subj. is consecutive: *qui* = *ut uos*.

**110–11 pacem . . . | oratis?** 'Do you ask me for peace with the dead?' The first word carries great emphasis, sustained by the alliteration with *peremptis*. Cf. 362 *pacem te poscimus omnes*. The double accus., of the thing asked and the person of whom it is asked, is normal with *oro* and similar verbs.

**oratis:** the final syllable is here 'lengthened', or treated as metrically 'heavy', in arsis before a caesura, a licence fairly frequent in hexameter verse though avoided by the elegists. Cf. 323 *amor et*, 469 *pater et*, and see Austin on 1.308.

**equidem** = *ego equidem*, as always in V. where it comes first in the sentence: 'for my part'. Cf. 1.576, 5.26, 9.207, 10.29, 12.931.

**uellem** 'I would have wished': the subj. is past potential.

**112 nec ueni:** Latin normally uses the pluperf. subj. in such sentences, just as English normally uses the past conditional: 'and I should not have come (=*nec uenissem*) if the fates had not ...' The use of the perf. indic. here heightens the vividness of the rhetoric: it may perhaps be seen as an extension of the common use of the indicative of *sum, possum,* etc., in an apodosis implying possibility: e.g. 4.18–19 *si non pertaesum thalami taedaeque fuisset,* | *huic uni forsan potui succumbere culpae, Georg.* 2.131–3 *ipsa ingens arbos faciemque simillima lauro,* | *et, si non alium late iactaret odorem,* | *laurus erat.* Cf. also 115, 117nn.

**fata ... dedissent:** a pervasive motif of the *Aen.* Cf. 7.122 *hic domus, haec patria est,* 8.39 *hic tibi certa domus,* 4.340–7 (Aen. tells Dido that if he had had his own way he would never have left Troy, but fate decreed otherwise).

**115 aequius ... fuerat** 'it would have been more fitting': cf. 117, 303 *fuerat melius,* and 112n.

**huic** is deictic and emphatic: '*this* death'.

**116 manu** is often used pleonastically with verbs of action (kill, attack, etc.) but is here perhaps more emphatic: 'if he plans to finish the war by force (rather than by negotiation) ...'

**117 his ... telis** 'then with these weapons it would have been more fitting for him to contend with me' (rather than with Pallas).

**118** 'Then he to whom the god or his own right arm gave life would have lived.' A highly rhetorical and epigrammatic line. Throughout this speech, Aen. proclaims his reluctance to engage in a civil war with the local tribes (113 *nec bellum cum gente gero,* and cf. 119 *miseris ... ciuibus*) and challenges Turnus: if there must be conflict, let it be between the two of them.

**uixet** = *uixisset*: these contracted forms are sometimes used by Lucretius and V. for metrical convenience: cf. 4.606 *exstinxem* = *exstinxissem,* 5.786 *traxe* = *traxisse.* See further Norden on 6.57 *derexti,* Austin on 1.201 *accestis.*

**119 supponite ... ignem:** for the burning of the dead cf. 6.223–4 *subiectam more parentum* | *auersi tenuere facem.*

**120–1** Cf. 2.1 *conticuere omnes intentique ora tenebant* (the same combination of silence and attention). For *conuersi ... oculos* cf. 12.172 *conuersi* *lumina*; in the present passage, *oculos* should be taken with both *conuersi* and *tenebant*.

**122** Drances appears only in *Aen.* xi. He is described at 336–41; see also Introd. 14–15. Out of hatred of Turnus rather than a true love of peace he opposes the war-party and emphasises for the reader Turnus' increasing isolation from the rest of the Latins.

**123–4 sic ore uicissim | orsa refert** 'began to speak in his turn'; also at 7.435–6 with the positions of *ore* and *orsa* reversed.

**orsa:** the substantive use of this participle, 'beginnings', is rare; in these two passages, and at 10.632, V. uses it to mean 'first words'. For the assonance *ore . . . orsa* cf. 42–3, 729, 830.

**124–6** It is a *donnée* of Aen.'s character as a good king that he excelled both in moral virtue (*pietas*) and in military prowess: cf. 291–2, and 1.544 *quo iustior alter | nec pietate fuit nec bello maior et armis.* Here the intention is to flatter: Drances is thinking of himself, not of Aeneas, and the emphasis of his words falls on the two first-person singular verbs, *aequem, mirer,* 'how am *I* to match your praises, where shall *I* start?', etc.

**125 quibus . . . aequem** 'with what praises am I to raise you to the skies?' For the hyperbole *aequare caelo* cf. 4.89 *aequataque machina caelo,* and for its figurative use, with *laudibus* etc., Livy 2.49.1 *Fabios ad caelum laudibus ferunt,* Tac. *Ann.* 4.34 *libro quo Catonem caelo aequauit.* Aen. was, of course, subsequently deified.

**126 iustitiaene . . . laborum:** the genitives are governed by *mirer* in imitation of Greek usage (after words of wondering, etc.). *belli* is gen. of definition.

**127 haec** 'these words of yours' (deictic).

**128 uiam:** cf. 10.49 *quaecumque uiam dederit Fortuna,* 10.113 *fata uiam inuenient.*

**128–9 te . . . Latino | iungemus regi:** this refers back to Latinus' offer of friendship with Aeneas made to the envoy Ilioneus at 7.263–4 *si iungi hospitio properat sociusque uocari, | adueniat –* an overture which Turnus has overruled.

**130–1** 'Yes, and (*quin et*: cf. 169) we shall even be glad to raise your mighty walls decreed by fate and carry on our shoulders the stones of Troy.' *quin et* = *quin etiam,* adding a further emphatic point.

**fatalis:** see 112, 232. *attollere moles*: cf. 2.185 *attollere molem* (of the wooden horse).

**133** In *Il.* 24.664–7 there is a truce lasting eleven days, 'and on the

twelfth we will do battle if necessary'. There is another truce in *Il.* VI:
see further Introd. 12–14.

**pace sequestra** 'with peace as mediator' (abl. absolute).

**134 mixtique** qualifies both *Teucri* and *Latini* (the ἀπὸ κοινοῦ
construction).

**135–8** Cf. 6.180–2 *sonat icta securibus ilex | fraxineaeque trabes cuneis et
fissile robur | scinditur, aduoluunt ingentis montibus ornos.* Both these descrip-
tions of the felling of forest-trees for the funeral pyre are modelled on
Ennius, who introduced it into Latin epic from Homer, *Il.* 23.110–22
(preparations for the funeral of Patroclus). Cf. *Ann.* 175–9:

> incedunt arbusta per alta, securibus caedunt,
> percellunt magnas quercus, exciditur ilex,
> fraxinus frangitur atque abies consternitur alta,
> pinus proceras peruortunt: omne sonabat
> arbustum fremitu siluai frondosai.

The survival of this passage, quoted by Macrobius, *Sat.* 6.2.27, offers,
in the words of Austin (n. on 6.179ff.) 'the rare opportunity of an
extended comparison' between V. and Ennius. Ennius uses far more
spondees, conveying an effect of massive blows and crashing timber. In
the present passage V. has retained Ennius' oak, ash and pine, and
added two indigenous Italian trees: the cedar (cf. the description of
Latinus' palace with its effigies *antiqua e cedro*, 7.178) and the *ornus* or
'manna ash' described by J. Sargeaunt, *Trees, shrubs and plants of Virgil*
(Oxford 1920) 93, as 'the typical hillside tree of central and S. Italy'.
For a full analysis of Ennius' lines see Skutsch 341–3, and for later
versions of the *topos* Williams, *TORP* 263.

**137–8** Another ex. of the need to construe Latin sentences as a whole:
*robora, cedrum* and *ornos* must all be taken as objects of both *scindere* and
*uectare*: see 19–21n.

**139–81** The funeral cortège arrives at Pallanteum and is greeted by
Evander. The reader will recall the closing scene of *Il.* XXIV in which
Priam brings Hector's body back to Troy.

**139 Fama** 'Rumour': cf. 4.173, 7.104, 8.544–5, 9.473–5 (where, as
here, Rumour brings the news of a young hero's death to his parent).

**140 Euandrum Euandrique:** the long, slow spondees of the repetition convey an effect of emptiness and dreariness.

**141** '(Rumour) which had only just now reported Pallas as victorious in Latium'. The line carries a sad and ironic emphasis: such are the changing fortunes of war. Servius pointed out that, since Pallas' *aristeia* lasted only one day, news of this would scarcely have had time to percolate through to Pallanteum, to be followed almost at once by this cruel reversal: cf. 10.507–8, where the poet apostrophises the dead Pallas as Homer had apostrophised Patroclus, *o dolor atque decus magnum rediture parenti, | haec te prima dies bello dedit, haec eadem aufert.*

**Latio:** locative ablative rather than dative.

**142 de more uetusto:** Servius has a long note on the Roman custom of carrying torches at funerals, which took place at night, perhaps in order to conceal the family's bereavement from public gaze. Cf. the description of Germanicus' funeral in Tac. *Agr.* 3.4.

**143–4 lucet ... agros** 'the way is lit up by the long line of torches making a wide path through the fields': a vivid picture. *late* should be taken with *longo ordine* as a variant of *longe lateque* 'far and wide', as at *Georg.* 3.477 *saltus longe lateque uacantis.*

**lucet uia longo:** for the rhythm of this type of line-ending, three successive disyllables yielding a conflict of ictus and accent in the fifth foot, cf. 170, 562, Gransden on 8.382.

**discriminat** 'divides', 'distinguishes'; a striking metaphor. The word occurs only here in V.

**147 incendunt clamoribus urbem:** for the metaphor (particularly appropriate here) cf. 10.895 *clamore incendunt caelum.* At 9.500 Euryalus' mother is said to be 'kindling lamentation' (*incendentem luctus*) as she mourns her son, and at 4.360 Aen. rebukes Dido for setting them both 'on fire' with her complaints (*desine meque tuis incendere teque querelis*).

This verse has a powerful, sombre tread, produced by the sequence of spondees, the (elided) key-word *maestam* and the measured assonance of the verb-endings.

**148 potis est:** for *potest* (archaism). V. has this form once in the *Georgics* and three times in the *Aeneid* (also at 3.671, 9.796).

**149–50 Pallanta** is the reading to be preferred here, with M², Page, Conington and Paratore. For the postposition of *super* after its accus., cf. 880, 10.384, 10.490, 10.893, and *supra* at 11.509–10. *Pallante*, read by most MSS and by Servius, seems to have come in by attraction to the adjacent abl. absolute, and through a misunderstanding of the meaning of *reposto*: the word refers to the setting down of the bier, not the stretching of Pallas upon it. The procession is halted when it reaches

the Arcadians coming to meet it, the bier is set down, and Evander falls
upon his son's body.

**151** The strong alliterative pattern, *u, u, x, u, x*, marks, as Page says,
'the convulsive sobs that choke his utterance.' For the metaphor in *uia*
cf. 7.533 *uocis iter*.

**uix tandem:** cf. 3.309; *tandem* emphasises the word it follows.

**151–81** Evander's lament for Pallas is both deeply felt and formally
constructed, with elaborate interlaced alliterative patterns, e.g. 155–60
*pr, d, d, pr, pr, pr, d, d, pr*. For the length, thirty lines, see Gransden, *Aen.
VIII* App. A, and O. A. W. Dilke, 'Do line totals in the *Aeneid* show a
preoccupation with significant number?', *C.Q.* N.S. 17 (1967) 322–7.

**152–3** 'This was not the promise you gave your father (when he
begged) that you would commit yourself more cautiously to cruel war.'
The echo of an earlier passage (v. 45) is characteristic of V., as is the
ellipse. Heyne placed a full stop at the end of 152 and explained *ut uelles*
as = *utinam uoluisses*, 'would that you had been willing', but this would
be very abrupt even if one allows that, in Heyne's words, *turbata oratio
dolore loquentis*. The reading *petenti* for *parenti*, mentioned by Servius, is,
as Page says, 'a good explanatory gloss'.

**uelles:** here, as elsewhere, *uolo* shades into a weakened auxiliary role.

**154–5** Theme and variation: *noua gloria in armis* and *praedulce decus
primo certamine* are exactly parallel, the second phrase amplifying the
first in accordance with V.'s favourite binary pattern. The emphasis
falls on *noua* and *primo*: Evander reflects sadly on the excitement and
novelty of a young man's first combat experience.

**quantum ... posset** 'how potent would be the effect (of)'.

**156–8 primitiae ... rudimenta ... uota precesque:** all
vocatives.

**propinqui** 'so near home'. Page well comments 'he had longed to
reap a harvest of fame, but the first-fruits were death: the lesson he had
learned was cruel and he had not to go far to learn it'.

**158–61** The grief of old men over sons slain in battle is a *topos* which
goes back to Homer's Priam, *Il.* 24.485–506; but Evander here articu-
lates a more specific cause of grief, his own survival: a similar sentiment
is expressed by Mezentius after the death of his son Lausus, 10.846–56.
There is a close parallel in Euripides, *Alc.* 939–40, where Admetus says:
ἐγὼ δ' ὃν οὐ χρῆν ζῆν, παρεὶς τὸ μόρσιμον, | λυπρὸν διάξω βίοτον, 'I,

who ought not to be alive, having outrun my destiny, shall live on in misery.'

**160 uiuendo uici** 'I have defeated my destiny by surviving.' For the alliterative phrase cf. Lucr. 1.202 *uiuendo uitalia uincere saecla.*

**161 restarem ut genitor:** the word-order places *genitor* in emphatic correspondence with *coniunx* at 158. For the postposition of *ut* see Norden Anh. iii 402–4.

**161–3** 'The Rutuli should have overwhelmed [*sc.* me] with their weapons as I followed the allied armies of Troy, I should have given *my* life [*ipse* emphasises the first person singular] and this funeral procession should be bringing back me, not Pallas.' The subjunctives are past jussives (or unfulfilled wishes): cf. 10.853–4, where Mezentius expressed similar sentiments over the body of his son: *debueram patriae poenas odiisque meorum:* | *omnis per mortis animam sontem ipse dedissem!*

**164 nec uos arguerim** 'not that I would blame you': potential subj., as at 10.185–6 *non ego te ...* | *transierim.*

**nec quas:** lines ending in two monosyllables are infrequent in V. Such lines do not necessarily involve any metrical irregularity, and there is none here (but cf. 170n.). Enjambment and hyperbaton (dislocation of word-order) combine to give these lines both flexibility and a forward-thrusting urgency.

**165–6 sors ... nostrae** 'that fate was assigned to me in my old age'. Evander does not blame the Trojans but accepts the fact that fate had doomed him to his present grief. *ista* is deictic: Evander points to Pallas' corpse.

**166–8** 'But if an untimely death did await him [as it did, hence the indicative] it will be a consolation to me that he died leading the Trojans into Latium after having first slain many Volsci.'

**166 quod si** 'but if': cf. 357, 434. *si* is elided eleven times in V.: Soubiran 410, 412.

**167 Volscorum milibus:** neither the proper name nor the number need be taken literally; Pallas did not kill only Volsci, and large round numbers are common in poetry.

**ante** is an adverb, qualifying the words it follows, cf. 1.198 *neque enim ignari sumus ante malorum*, where *ante* goes with *sumus.*

**169 quin** 'Yes, and': cf. 130.

**170 quam ... quam ... quam** 'than the one with which (*quo ...*

*dignantur* must be supplied) Aeneas and the great chiefs and the whole army now honour you'. The repetitions emphasise Pallas' worth. The metre of the line is unusual, not because of the final monosyllables (see 164n.) but because these are preceded by two disyllables, so that the effect resembles that at 143, 562.

**171** For the structure of this line cf. 598.

**Tyrrhenique ... Tyrrhenum:** the repetition replaces the second *-que*, a figure which appears only in the second half of the *Aen.*: cf. 641, 7.75, 10.313.

**172** A problematical line. The subject of *ferunt* may be either (1) the Trojan chiefs (inferred from v.171) in which case *eorum* is to be understood as the antecedent of *quos* (cf. 84, where Aen. orders the Trojan leaders to carry the enemy trophies in the procession); or (2) the enemies slain by Pallas, in which case *quos* = *ii quos* and *ferunt* cannot be taken literally. Conington, Page and Williams all prefer the second interpretation, but Heyne preferred the first, and this seems to be the one the implied reader would have been most likely to 'hear' when the passage was read aloud. It is interesting that when Heyne glosses the second interpretation he produces what is virtually a paraphrase of the first, *tropaea magna ducuntur in pompa funebri eorum qui a filio meo caesi fuere.* Fitzgerald's rendering neatly dissolves the 'undecidability' of the line: 'Men to whom / Your sword-arm dealt out death are here as trophies, / Great ones.'

**dat:** present tense used to denote a past action whose effect remains valid: cf. 9.266 *quem dat Sidonia Dido* ( = 'the gift of'). Here the idiom is helped by the influence of a second verb in the present tense, as at 8.141 *idem Atlas generat caeli qui sidera tollit.*

**173–4** 'You too, Turnus, would now be standing there, a huge tree-trunk decked in arms, if he [Pallas] had your years and strength to match.' For the tree-trunk as trophy see 5–11n. Evander's thoughts turn naturally to the greatest prize of all, the one which eluded Pallas.

**armis:** Bentley emended this to *aruis* to avoid repetition with 175, but such repetitions are common enough in V.: see Austin on 2.505. *armis* occurs at the end of the line 23 times in book XI, *in armis* also at 154, 308, 464, 710, 769, 910. For *stare in armis* cf. 9.581, 12.938.

**robur ab annis:** for this 'ablative of origin' see Mackail App. A and cf. Lucr. 2.51 *fulgorem ab auro.* For the postposition of *si* cf. 201n.

**175 Turne. sed:** an unusually bold sense-break in the first foot of the line: cf. 10.73, 10.777. In the last books of the *Aen.* V.'s treatment of the hexameter becomes increasingly bold and flexible, especially in respect of enjambment and the use of strong sense-breaks early in the line: see further Gransden, *Aen. VIII* 47, Introd. 31.

**infelix** 'in my wretchedness' (predicative).

**176 regi:** Aen., for whom the rest of the speech is intended.

**177–9** Evander's words effectively seal Turnus' fate. However reluctantly (and he *is* reluctant), Aen. must eventually discharge this debt of honour.

**177 quod** 'as to why': a loose connective like *quod si.* 'The reason I prolong a life I hate is your right hand' [i.e. the instrument of vengeance] which you see owes Turnus to son and father alike.'

**178 dextera:** echoing 172. Pallas' sword-arm has performed valiantly, vanquished only by the superior strength and experience of Turnus. Now it is up to Aen.

**179 debere:** cf. 10.442–3 *soli mihi Pallas | debetur* 'Pallas is mine alone'.

**179–80 meritis ... locus** 'this is the only place left open to you for [the exercise of your] worth and fortune.' E.'s peroration rises to hyperbole. Only the killing of T. can crown Aen.'s glory.

**180–1 non ... imos** 'I do not seek this pleasure for my own life, nor would that be right, but to carry [the news of it] to my son in the underworld.' *uitae* is in exact and emphatic correspondence to *gnato* ('not for me but for him'). *quaero* is here constr. first with an accus., then with an infin.; *gaudia* is also to be taken as the obj. of *perferre*, replacing the more usual 'message' or 'news' (cf. 825).

**182–224** The burning of the dead. Cf. Homer *Il.* 7.422–32, 24.783–7.

**182–3** The motif of the return of dawn, bringing labour to mortals, goes back to Greek literature: see Gransden, 'Lente currite, noctis equi', in *Creative imitation in Latin literature*, ed. D. West and A. J. Woodman (Cambridge 1979) 157–71.

**miseris mortalibus** (cf. Lucr. 5.944) =Homer's δειλοῖσι βροτοῖσι.

**atque:** except for Horace, the Augustan poets usually elide this word. V. has 35 instances of the unelided form, all but eight of them in the second half of the poem (including two striking instances in which the word ends the line, 12.355, 12.615); it occurs unelided in the fifth foot ten times in the *Aen.*, six of these instances being in the last three books

(10.51, 10.535, 11.183, 11.668, 11.725, 12.332). Here and at 725 (= 1.254) the word is part of a formulaic phrase. See further Axelson 84; Fordyce on 7.317; M. Platnauer, *C.Q.* 42 (1948) 91–3; E. J. Kenney on *Moretum* 44 (Bristol Classical Press 1984).

**labores:** V. uses this word to denote heroic effort, especially of Aen.'s 'Herculean' labours (see e.g. 1.10, 1.241, 1.330, 1.460, 1.597, etc.); here it is used to convey a sense of the harshness of the human condition which can be traced back to Hesiod: cf. 10.758–9 *di Iouis in tectis iram miserantur inanem | amborum et tantos mortalibus esse labores.*

**184 Tarchon:** an Etruscan king, mythical founder of V.'s birthplace Mantua. On the antiquarian traditions about him see Gransden on 8.506, Galinsky 142, Grant 74. He agrees to an alliance with Aen. at 10.146–54 and is prominent in the cavalry engagement described later in bk XI (725–58).

**curuo in litore** must be taken ἀπὸ κοινοῦ, with both Aeneas and Tarchon.

**185–6 suorum:** with *corpora*, not with *patrum*.

**more patrum** 'in the manner of his ancestors' (cf. 6.223 *more parentum*). The funeral rites of the Trojans and Etruscans are now described in language full of epic grandeur. Cf. the account of Misenus' funeral rites, 6.212–35.

**188–9 ter ... ter:** cf. Homer, *Il.* 23.13.

**decurrere:** Roman technical term for ritual procession, cf. Livy 25.17.5, Tac. *Ann.* 2.7.

**190 lustrauere in equis** (= 5.578) 'rode round'. *lustrare* means to process round in an act of purification: see W. Warde Fowler, *The death of Turnus* (Oxford 1919) 96–8. This is an amplification of *decurrere* in the preceding sentence: V. is describing a single ritual act of triple circumlustration on horseback.

**191 spargitur ... sparguntur:** the anaphora serves both for emotional emphasis and as a connective device: cf. 8.161 *mirabarque duces Teucros, mirabar et ipsum.* The present line is modelled on Homer, *Il.* 23.15 δεύοντο ψάμαθοι, δεύοντο δε τεύχεα φωτῶν | δάκρυσι.

**192** = 2.313, except that *it caelo* is substituted for *exoritur*. The line is grandly alliterative and onomatopoeic and rounds off the first part of the description of the funeral (epiphonema).

**it caelo:** also at 5.451: the dative usage (for *in caelum*) also occurs at 206 and cf. 6.126 *facilis descensus Auerno* ('*id est ad Auernum*', Servius).

**tubarum:** trumpets were used in Roman funerals, cf. Hor. *Sat.* 1.6.44.

**193–6 alii ... pars:** for the use of *pars* as a variant cf. *Ecl.* 1.65, and for other exx. see *OLD* s.v. 3b. In such constructions *pars* often takes a plural verb, e.g. at 6.218–22, 6.642–4. Here a verb (*coniciunt igni*) must be supplied.

**194** The ritual burning of shields captured from the enemy was supposed to have been introduced by Tarquinius Priscus after a victory over the Sabines (Livy 1.37.5). Cf. 8.562.

**195 feruentisque:** a conventional epithet for chariot wheels (cf. Hor. *C.* 1.1.4), which some edd. have found inappropriate here, but it could be argued that the metaphor is heightened rather than weakened by *coniciunt igni*.

**nota** 'familiar': cf. 6.221 *uelamina nota*, which Servius glosses as *ipsi cara* and Heyne as *quibus ipse, dum uiueret, usus erat*. Here, however, the word may mean that such offerings were a familiar feature of funerals.

**196 non felicia:** litotes. These are the weapons of their own dead, which failed to protect them.

**197–9** The sacrifice of sheep and oxen is Homeric (*Il.* 23.30–2, 23.166), the sacrifice of pigs is not (see *Aen.* 8.84–5).

**197 Morti:** dat. after *mactantur*, cf. 8.84–5, Livy 9.40 *eos se Orco mactare dictitans*. V. does not elsewhere personify Mors, but cf. Hor. *C.* 1.4.13 *pallida Mors aequo pulsat pede pauperum tabernas*. In no other passage in the *Aen.* would the personification be more profoundly appropriate. Mackail prints *morti* as an archaic ablative, like *sorti* at 9.271 ('are sacrificed in death'), arguing that the phrase is probably Ennian and that a personification (first proposed by Servius) is untenable, though he does not say why. The dative usage is further supported by 10.662 *obuia multa uirum demittit corpora morti*.

**200–1 ardentis ... busta** 'they watch their comrades as they burn (*ardentis*: predicative), and keep guard over the half-burned pyres': a typical Virgilian binary sentence, the second colon a variation on the first.

**semustaque ... busta:** a striking assonance. *semusta = semiusta*, scanned as a trisyllable (synizesis): cf. 8.194 *semihominis*, 12.356 *semianimi*.

**201–2 neque ... aptum** 'nor can they tear themselves away until dewy night revolves the sky studded with blazing stars'. The heavens were regarded as consisting of two hemispheres, one light, the other dark, which revolve, bringing alternate day and night. The noble phrase is from Ennius: cf. *Ann.* 348 *nox processit stellis ardentibus apta*, 27, 145 *caelum . . . stellis fulgentibus aptum*, whence Lucr. 6.357-8 *stellis fulgentibus apta | . . . caeli domus.* Some edd. prefer the reading *fulgentibus* in the present passage, to avoid a repetition of *ardentis* (200), which they assume to be undesirable, but poets often exploit repetition effectively: here we move from the blazing corpses to the blazing stars, from man-made fires to the fires of heaven; the camera tracks away to form a magnificent close.

**donec:** for the postponed connective cf. 174, Norden Anh. iii 402-4; for the placing of a 'colourless' word at the end of the line cf. 282, 374, 471, 509, 816, Introd. 31.

**203 Nec minus:** a transitional formula, cf. 8.465; sometimes with *interea*, e.g. 12.107.

**204-5 partim | . . . partim:** for the repetition at the end of two consecutive lines cf. 7.653-4 *esset*, 9.544-5 *Helenor.* For *partim . . . partim* cf. 10.330-1. The meaning here is that some bodies were buried on the spot, others returned to their home towns, but that large numbers of the unidentifiable dead were burned where they lay.

**207-9** These lines, with their slow spondees and strong alliterative pattern, offer a vivid and moving image of the desolation and meaninglessness of war. For the unidentified bodies cf. Homer, *Il.* 7.424, and for the fires burning on all sides cf. *Il.* 1.52.

**207 confusaeque:** *-que* is epexegetic: it does not add anything new but explains and amplifies *cetera*.

**208 nec numero nec honore** 'unnumbered and unnamed'.

**uasti** 'waste' (not 'vast'): cf. 8.8 *uastant.*

**210** For the time-span of the narrative see Introd. 9-10. For the structure of the line cf. 3.589 ( =4.7) *umentemque Aurora polo dimouerat umbram.*

**211-12** Cf. the description of the dying down of the pyres at the cremation of Misenus, 6.226-8 *postquam conlapsi cineres et flamma quieuit, | reliquias uino et bibulam lauere fauillam, | ossaque lecta cado texit Coryaenus aëno.* In that passage V. closely follows Homeric models (*Il.* 23.250, 24.791-4). Here the dying down of the fire and the ritual quenching of the ashes are omitted; V. merely says that they raked out the ashes and bones and piled earth on them.

**211 maerentes:** cf. 216 *maerentum.*

**confusa:** cf. 207 *confusae.*

**ruebant** 'levelled': cf. 9.516 *immanem Teucri molem uoluuntque ruuntque,* *Georg.* 1.105 *cumulosque ruit male pinguis harenae.*

**213 praediuitis:** the word occurs only here in V.

**214** A grandly rhetorical and formally constructed line, with an echoing assonance of *prae* from the previous line, and the 'enclosing word-order' of the last four words emphasised by alliteration.

**fragor:** often applied by V. to natural phenomena; here it refers to the sound of human voices, cf. 5.228.

**215–16** Cf. the description of the throngs of the dead, 6.306–8 *matres atque uiri defunctaque corpora uita | magnanimum heroum, pueri innuptaeque puellae, | impositique rogis iuuenes ante ora parentum.* Here V. describes the mourning women and children. *miserae* is to be taken with both *matres* and *nurus* (the ἀπὸ κοινοῦ construction). *nurus* refers to unmarried girls, cf. 2.501.

**217 dirum exsecrantur bellum:** it is to the indigenous Latins, mainly at peace till the Trojans came, that V. gives his most powerful anti-war sentiments.

**Turnique hymenaeos:** V. occasionally admits a quadrisyllabic word (usually of Greek origin) at the end of the line, cf. 69, 355, 4.99, 4.316.

**218–19** 'They tell *him* to take arms, *him* to decide the war, since he is the one who claims the kingdom and leadership of Italy.'

**ipsum ... ipsumque:** *-que* emphasises the repetition, as in the phrase *iam iamque* (12.754, 12.940).

**decernere ferro:** so Ennius, *Ann.* 132: also used by V. at *Aen.* 12.282, 12.695; cf. *Georg.* 3.218.

**qui** with the subj. = *quippe qui.*

**220 ingrauat:** a rare word, only here in V.

**220–1 solumque ... solum:** picking up *ipsum ... ipsum* from 218.

**223 obumbrat** 'protects him': a striking metaphor. The word is used in its literal sense at 12.578.

### 225–444 The Latin war-council; the report of the envoy Venulus

**226–7** This is the return of the embassy of Venulus despatched by the Latins (see 8.9–17), to seek military aid from Diomedes, the Greek hero and survivor of Troy, who has settled at Argyripa (Arpi).

**226 super** 'on top of everything' ( = *insuper*): cf. 2.71, 7.462.

**227–30** A summary of Diomedes' response (later given in full, verbatim) is here given in *oratio obliqua*.

**227 nihil ... actum** (sc. *esse*) 'nothing has been achieved'.

**230 petendum:** the gerund with accus. object in place of the more usual gerundive: cf. Lucr. 1.111 *aeternas quoniam poenas in morte timendumst.* Most MSS read *petendam* here, but Servius attests the gerund and it should be retained ('difficilior lectio potior').

**231–5** Latinus is overcome by deep sadness and an overwhelming conviction that Aen. is the destined leader of Italy. When he speaks in the council (302–35) it is for the first time since 7.594–9; there, in moving words (*frangimur, heu, fatis ... ferimurque procella*) he warned the Latins that they, and especially Turnus, must bear the guilt of the coming war. After that brief speech, he relinquished the leadership (*rerum ... reliquit habenas*), leaving Turnus and the war-party in effective control.

**232–5** 'The wrath of the gods as shown in the sight of fresh-dug graves warns him that Aeneas is sent by fate and by the clear will of heaven.' The word-order places heavy emphasis on Aen. the man of destiny: 232 is marked by its spondaic opening and alliteration of *f*.

**fatalem:** Aen. is not elsewhere given this epithet, which is hardly ever applied to persons (see *OLD* s.v.), but the motif of the fate-sent hero dominates the poem: cf. 7.255, 7.272, 8.512. *fatalem* may also carry a suggestion of its other meaning, 'deadly', and the reader may recall the wooden horse from 2.237 *fatalis machina*.

**233 -que** is epexegetic: the graves are evidence of divine anger.

**234–5** 'And so he convenes a great council of his chiefs, summoned by his command.'

**primosque suorum | imperio accitos:** the natural way to translate this hendiadys is by using the genitive; or one could say that *-que* is epexegetic; *cogit* repeats the sense of *accitos*. *cogere* is the normal verb for convening a meeting of the senate, cf. 304, 460 and see *OLD* s.v. 4.

**236 olli:** the archaism is appropriate; the whole passage has an Ennian ring.

**conuenere fluuntque:** theme and variation.

**238 sceptris** 'authority', cf. 9.9, 10.852; the reader will hear in the Greek word echoes of the sceptre held by the Homeric heroes in council, especially Agamemnon, something of whose Iliadic role is assumed by

Virgil's Latinus, especially at 12.206–11, where he actually wields the sceptre. Cf. Gransden, *VI* 196–8.

**haud laeta:** litotes. The heavily spondaic line again emphasises the gloom and despondency of the occasion.

**239 Aetola:** Diomedes came from Aetolia and became king of Argos, see 243, 246–7.

**241 linguis:** instrumental ablative.

**242 farier:** the (metrically convenient) archaic form of the infinitive *fari:* cf. 4.493 *accingier*, 7.70 *dominarier*, 8.493 *defendier*, 9.231 *admittier*.

**243** The first-hand account by Venulus of his embassy's reception at Argyripa, the greater part of which (vv. 252–93) consists of the actual words of Diomedes. For further comment on this passage see Introd. 15–16. See also 245n.

**243 Vidimus** is emphatic: the envoys have carried out their mission.

**245** 'We have grasped the hand that overthrew Ilium.' Aen.'s respect for Diomedes' valour is mentioned several times in the poem: see Introd. 16.

**246–7 Argyripam:** Diomedes was still building (*condebat*) this city, named for his homeland of Argos, in land given him by Daunus, whom he had helped to victory against the Messapians.

**Gargani ... Iapygis** 'Iapygian Garganus': a poetic periphrasis referring to that part of Apulia (Iapygia) in or near which Mt Garganus was situated.

**248** = 1.520.

**copia** 'opportunity'; at 378 it means 'store'.

**250** 'who had attacked us and what reason had drawn [us] to Arpi'. The indirect questions are dependent on *docemus*.

**Arpos** 'to Arpi': another name for Argyripa, cf. 10.28–9 *atque iterum in Teucros Aetolis surgit ab Arpis* | *Tydides*.

**252–3** V. sometimes depicted the blessings of peace enjoyed by the aboriginal Italians as a prolongation of the 'golden age' when Saturn ruled over Latium: see 7.45–6, 8.324–5, Gransden, *Aen. VIII* 36–8.

**o fortunatae:** cf. the famous passage on the farmer's life at *Georg.* 2.458ff. (*o fortunatos nimium ...*) with its emphasis on *secura quies*. The poetic forms *Ausonia, Ausonii* carry the same kind of nostalgic resonance.

**fortunatae ... fortuna:** a striking ex. of word-play ('figura etymologica'): the effect is to emphasise a mutation from good to ill fortune.

**quietos** 'in your peace': predicative.

**254 suadetque ... bella?** 'and persuades you to risk the unknown challenge of war?': *bella* is plural for singular; *ignota* repeats the sense of *quietos*.

**255–8 quicumque ... omnes:** an eloquent ex. of enclosing word-order: 'all of us who outraged the fields of Ilium ... have paid the price ... to the last man'.

**uiolauimus** is used to describe the violation of something sacred (Homer's 'holy Ilium'): cf. 277.

**(mitto ... uiros)** 'I pass over all the sufferings endured in battle beneath those high walls, and all those whom famous Simois covers.'

**exhausta:** literally 'drunk to the dregs': for the metaphor cf. *Macbeth* 5.5.13 'I have supped full with horrors.'

**premat:** subj., for the number of the dead can never be known.

**ille:** emphatically deictic: cf. 261 *ille*.

**259 uel ... manus** 'a crew even Priam might feel pity for'. *manus* is in apposition to (*nos*) *omnes* and completes the long 'enclosed' sentence.

**259–60 scit ... et ... -que:** a typically Virgilian tricolon (theme and two variations). In revenge for the violation by Ajax of her priestess Cassandra, Minerva (Pallas Athene) sent a storm which shipwrecked the returning Greeks off the Euboean promontory of Caphereus, where the king, Nauplius, hung out false lights to avenge his son Palamedes, put to death on a false charge by Odysseus at Troy. There is thus a double revenge-motif in this densely allusive passage, which expands the idea of *poenas expendimus*: one way or another, through agencies both human and divine, Troy has had its revenge on Greece.

The storm is referred to by Homer, *Od.* 1.326–7, 2.132–5; cf. also *Aen.* 1.39–41, where Juno says *Pallasne exurere classem | Argiuum atque ipsos potuit summergere ponto | unius ob noxam et furias Aiacis Oilei?* For Palamedes cf. *Aen.* 2.82 with Servius' n., and W. B. Stanford, *The Ulysses theme* (Oxford 1963, repr. Ann Arbor 1968) 96.

**260 sidus:** storms were thought by the ancients to be associated with the stars: cf. 12.451–5.

**Euboicae ... Caphereus** 'the avenging rocks of Euboean Caphereus' (hendiadys).

**261 illa:** cf. 257 *ille*.

**abacti** refers both to Menelaus and to Ulysses. Menelaus' adventures on the island of Pharos, '*nunc partem Alexandriae*' (Servius), are recounted by him in *Od.* 4.351–592: Proteus was the sea-god whom he ambushed there and forced to prophesy to him. For Ulysses and the Cyclops see *Od.* 9.187–92.

**262 Protei:** scanned as two syllables by synizesis.

**adusque** 'right up to'.

**columnas:** the word suggests, as Page points out, a contrast with the pillars of Hercules at the other (western) end of the world. *OLD* refers to Pliny, *N.H.* 6.199 *rubro mare nauigantes ... non posse propter ardores ultra quasdam columnas – ita appellantur paruae insulae – prouehi.*

**263 Cyclopas:** Greek accusative.

**264 referam** 'shall I refer to ...': the rhetorical figure known as paralipsis. *uersa* must be understood from *uersos* with *regna* (the ἀπὸ κοινοῦ construction). Neoptolemus ( = Pyrrhus), son of Achilles, killed Priam at the palace altar, an act of sacrilege recalled by Aen. in his account to Dido of the last night of Troy (2.526–58); according to Greek tradition, Neoptolemus was himself slain by Orestes at Apollo's altar at Delphi: see 3.332 and Williams's n.

**264–5** Idomeneus returning from Troy to Crete was caught in a storm and vowed that if he were saved he would sacrifice whatever he first saw on landing. This proved to be his own son; he fulfilled his vow, but a pestilence visited the land and he was forced into exile: see 3.122 and Williams's n.

**265** The Locri went to Troy with Ajax son of Oileus and were in the shipwreck off Euboea referred to above, 259–60. Some of them survived and settled in N. Africa, but nothing further seems to be known about this.

**266** A suitably grand and symmetrical verse describes Agamemnon, the climactic figure in this series of vignettes. His fate, the most notorious of any suffered by the returning Greeks, dominates the opening of the *Odyssey.*

**268 oppetiit** 'met his death': for the absolute usage cf. 12.543, 12.640.

**deuictam ... adulter** 'the adulterer lay in wait for Asia's defeat'. Servius preferred the reading *deuicta Asia* (abl. absolute); *subsedit* would then be intransitive: 'the adulterer lay in wait at Asia's fall' (Fitzgerald). In either sense the word is rare: see *OLD* s.v. 2, where the common editorial explanation of *deuictam Asiam* ( = 'the conqueror of Asia') is followed. But Page, in an excellent n. on this difficult line, argues that if V. had wanted to write *uictorem Asiae* he could perfectly well have done so, and that what he meant by *deuictam Asiam* was the hour of Asia's defeat: i.e. Aegisthus waited till the moment of Agamemnon's triumph to strike him down. See further Quinn 389–90.

**269 inuidisse deos** 'to think that the gods grudged . . .': accus. and infin. of exclamation as at 1.37–8, which Mynors punctuates as an exclamation, as do some edd. here. For the constr. with *ut* cf. 42–3 n. Diomedes' outburst is perhaps deliberately abrupt: the fate of Agamemnon prompts him to thoughts about his own experiences.

**270 coniugium:** for the unmetrical *coniugem*, cf. 2.579, Catullus 68.107.

**Calydona:** Greek accus. Diomedes' family originated in Calydon, whence his father Tydeus migrated to Argos.

**271–4** The metamorphosis of Diomedes' companions into birds is also treated, at much greater length, by Ovid, *Met.* 14.483–511. There too Diomedes himself is speaking, and in both passages he explains the portent as a punishment for his impious wounding of Venus at Troy (*Il.* 5.334–42). Servius says that V. altered the traditional story, in which the men were changed after D.'s death; it is much more effective to suggest that D. himself witnessed the phenomenon.

**272 et** 'as': epexegetic or explanatory.

**273 aues** 'as birds': predicative.

**275–6** 'Such disasters, indeed, were only to be expected now, ever since that fatal hour when . . .'

**adeo:** an intensive particle emphasising the word it follows, cf. 314, 487, and contrast 369 (n.) For *sperare* = 'expect' (not 'hope') cf. 1.543 and Conway's n.

**277** The striking alliteration of *u* emphasises the notorious act of impiety.

**278 ne . . . ne:** for the emphatic constr. cf. 6.832 *ne, pueri, ne tanta animis adsuescite bella*; 12.72 *ne quaeso, ne me lacrimis neue omine tanto | prosequere in duri certamina Martis euntem.*

**279–80 post eruta . . . | Pergama** 'after the destruction of Troy'. This use of the past participle is a common Latin idiom, as in the phrase *post urbem conditam*, and cf. 308n.

**280 nec . . . malorum** 'nor do I remember past evils with any pleasure'. The enclosing word-order is characteristically Virgilian, the two cola forming a single idea. *-ue* is sometimes used after a negative to link two closely related words: see *OLD* s.v. 2 and cf. 7.805 *non illa colo*

*calathisue Mineruae | femineas adsueta manus*. Here, *laetor* goes so closely
with *memini* as to operate virtually as an adverb and form a hendiadys.
As Conington well notes, 'it was not that he did not remember the war,
but that he took no pleasure in the remembrance'. This helps the
construction, in which the normal genitive after *memini* is extended to
*laetor* (*OLD* s.v. 1b).

**282 tela aspera contra:** the anastrophe of disyllabic prepositions
is quite usual in V. *contra* occurs at the end of the line five times in the
first half of the *Aen.*, fifteen times in the second half.

**283 quantus:** a bold enjambment; the word occurs only here at the
end of a line in the *Aen.* The effect is to throw immense emphasis on
Aen.'s towering presence in the field. The alliterative pattern of *t* and
*qu* is conspicuous in this and the following line.

**285–7** Cf. *Il.* 2.371–4, where Agamemnon tells Nestor that if he had
ten counsellors like him 'then would Priam's city soon bend beneath
our hands, captive and laid waste'.

**ultro ... fatis** 'then would the Trojan have actually reached the
Argive cities, and Greece would now be grieving at the reversal of
fortune'. For *ultro* cf. 2.192–4 *sin manibus uestris uestram ascendisset in
urbem,* | [sc. the wooden horse] *ultro Asiam magno Pelopea ad moenia bello* |
*uenturam.*

**Inachias:** a general word for Argive, or Greek, from Inachus king
of Argos: the metonymy is perhaps, as Williams suggests, specially
appropriate to the speaker's connection with Argos.

**Dardanus** 'the Trojan', collective singular: cf. 10.238 *Etrusco.*

**288–90** 'Whatever stalemate there was at the stubborn walls of
Troy, it was due to Hector's and Aeneas' right hand that a Greek
victory was delayed and dragged its feet until the tenth year.'

**quidquid** 'to whatever extent' (internal accus.). The emphasis in
these lines falls strongly on the phrase *Hectoris Aeneaeque manu.* For the
personification of *uictoria* cf. 436.

For the sentiment of these lines, that it was Hector and Aeneas who
delayed the Greek victory at Troy, cf. 9.154–5 *haud sibi cum Danais rem
faxo et pube Pelasga | esse ferant, decimum quos distulit Hector in annum.* Turnus
is speaking there, so he naturally ignores Aeneas' part in the war, but
the whole of his speech is relevant: Turnus had given reasons why the
Trojans could be beaten, while Diomedes gives reasons for refusing a
second engagement. Cf. also 2.197–8, where Aen. tells Dido that Si-

non's treachery achieved what ten years, a thousand ships and the combined prowess of Diomedes and Achilles could not accomplish: the defeat of Troy.

**292** Aen.'s reputation for *pietas* is first mentioned by Homer, *Il.* 20.298, though Hector is also famous for that quality (*Il.* 24.66–70). See further N. Horsfall, C.Q. N.S. 29 (1979) 372–90. For the idea that the right hand, the sword hand, ought rather to be held out in friendship, cf. 12.311 *at pius Aeneas dextram tendebat inermem.*

**293 qua datur** 'to the extent that it is allowed': i.e. while you still have the chance.

**concurrant:** jussive subj. after *cauete*: 'take care that they do not meet'.

**294–5** Venulus completes his report in a couplet heavy and formal with spondees. For the diplomatically formal repetition of the title *rex* cf. 8.17.

**magno ... bello** 'in so great a war', abl. 'of attendant circumstance': Hofmann–Szantyr 114–19, Palmer 300–3.

**296 Vix ea ... -que** 'scarcely had they finished speaking when ...': for the ellipse cf. 12.154. For the paratactic constr. *uix ... -que*, in which *-que = cum,* cf. 2.692 *uix ea fatus erat senior, subitoque fragore | intonuit laeuum ...*

**297–9** For this simile Knauer compares *Il.* 2.144–8 (after Agamemnon's speech the assembly is shaken as the sea by winds) but the resemblance is purely formal. Here the effect of the envoy's speech is to produce a confused and excited murmur like the noise of a river among rocks: the simile is carefully composed with striking alliterative and onomatopoeic effects (repetition of *r*, the echo *rapidos ... crepitantibus*) and is 'framed' between *turbata ora* (296–7) *trepida ora* (300).

**300 trepida:** continuing the onomatopoeic effect of *crepitantibus* in the simile. The adj. expresses excitement, not fear: cf. 453. The elision (of *-a*) at the end of the fourth foot is uncommon: Soubiran 536–7.

**301 praefatus diuos:** Servius refers to the ancient practice of prefacing an oration with a prayer, found in the speeches of Cato and the Gracchi and made mock of by Cicero.

**302–35** Latinus' speech. He proposes a peace-treaty with the Trojans, but avoids direct confrontation with Turnus (312 *nec quemquam incuso*). For the length of the speech (34 lines) cf. 152–81 n. and for its content see further Introd. 16–17.

**302 summa de re** 'concerning our present crisis': cf. 2.322 and

Austin's n. and 9.199 *summis ... rebus*. Latinus says he could have wished for a decision before things had reached their present pass, not now, with the enemy actually besieging the walls. His first word, *ante*, carries great emphasis and is answered by *non tempore tali*.

**303 fuerat melius:** cf. 115n.

**305–7** 'This is an appalling war, fellow-citizens, we are waging with men of divine race, and unbeaten powers, whom no battles weary and who even when defeated do not give up the fight.' The paradox that the Trojans, though defeated, remain unconquered is developed at length as a *topos* by Hor. *C.* 4.4.53–68.

**inuictisque ... uicti:** cf. Ennius, *Ann.* 344–5 [Pergama] *quae neque Dardaniis campis potuere perire | nec cum capta capi nec cum combusta cremari*, more closely imitated by V. in Juno's great outburst against Trojan survival at 7.293–6 *heu stirpem inuisam, et fatis contraria nostris | fata Phrygum! num Sigeis occumbere campis, | num capti potuere capi? num incensa cremauit | Troia uiros?* See also Wigodsky 70.

**importunum:** a strong word, used by V. elsewhere only of birds of ill omen (e.g. 12.864).

**308–9** 'If you have had any hope of getting the military support of the Aetolians, put it aside. Our only hope is in ourselves; and you see how inadequate that is.' These vv. are marked by repeated elisions (*quam ... Aetolum ... quam*) and are broken up into plain abrupt statements with two ellipses of *est*. Latinus puts the blunt facts before the council.

**308 ascitis ... in armis:** for this use of the past participle cf. 279–80n.

**309 ponite** is scanned as a dactyl before *sp-*: the irregularity is helped by the full stop (Allen 140). 3.270 *nemorosa Zacynthos* is not a true parallel, since the Greek word could not be fitted into a hexameter unless preceded by a short syllable.

**310–11** 'As for the rest of our fortunes, the ruins in which they lie are clearly visible and tangible.' *sunt omnia* is attracted to agree with *cetera*, the regular constr. being *est omnino* (sc. *ruina*). The epic phrase *perculsa ruina* contrasts effectively with 311, which consists entirely of *communia uerba*: V.'s liking for ordinary words was remarked in the ancient *Life* of the poet: see Gransden, *Aen. VIII* 43.

**314 nunc adeo:** the intensifier (see 275–6n.) emphasises the transition: 'That's all past history, but now ...'

**315** For the structure of this line cf. 6.759, 8.50.

**316 est:** the usual signifier for an ecphrasis or *descriptio loci*: cf. 522. V. here alludes to the tradition, preserved by Cato, that Latinus assigned land to the Trojans: see Introd. 16, Heinze 172. The geography of this and similar passages describing early Latium is somewhat obscure: the Aurunci, Rutuli and Sicani are mentioned together at 7.795, on which see Fordyce's n. The Sicani are also mentioned by Evander in his account of the earliest settlement of Latium: see Gransden on 8.328–9.

**317 super usque** = *usque super*.

**318–19 duros | ... pascunt** 'plough the stubborn hills and graze the wildest parts'. For *exercent uomere collis* cf. 7.798, a passage V. has already recalled (above, 316n.) in referring to the local tribes. Servius, in his n. on this passage, suggests that Latinus is trying to minimise the value of his gift; Servius suggests that he is thinking of the farmers who would be dispossessed. But the words are in any case appropriate to V.'s Italians, a tough breed *patiens operum paruoque adsueta* (9.607).

**320 et** 'including' (epexegetic).

**321 cedat amicitiae Teucrorum** 'be yielded up to our Trojan friends' (i.e. to win their friendship).

**323 amor:** for the 'lengthening' of the second syllable, see 110–11n., 12.13, 668.

**325 possuntque** 'and (if) it lies in their power', which of course it does not, for fate has decreed otherwise.

**326** Aen. had started his voyage with twenty ships (1.381) of which a mere seven (*uix septem*, 1.383) survived the storm with which the poem began; these had been transformed into sea-nymphs by Cybele, in accordance with a promise by Jupiter, to save them from being set fire to by Turnus (9.22–122).

**330–5** The language of treaty-making is formal and Roman.

**330 qui ... firment:** relative clause of purpose, here preceding its grammatical antecedent *oratores*.

**foedera firment:** cf. 12.212 *firmabant foedera*, Ennius, *Ann.* 32 *foedusque feri bene firmum*.

**331 oratores** 'ambassadors'.

**332** For the olive-branch as a symbol of peace cf. 101, 8.116 *paciferaeque manu ramum praetendit oliuae*.

**placet** 'we propose': the usual verb for senatorial and other official decisions.

**333 munera** 'as gifts' (predicative), in apposition to *talenta, sellam, trabeam.*

**334 regni ... insignia nostri** 'our royal emblems' (literally 'the emblems of our royalty'). A throne and a robe are among the gifts mentioned by Livy (27.4.8) as having been sent by the Romans to the Numidian prince Syphax.

**335 in medium** 'together'.

**336–42** Drances has already appeared briefly at 122–31, but V. now describes him in detail. For a discussion of his character and his role in book XI, see Introd. 14–15.

**336 idem infensus** 'hostile as ever'.

**337** 'Smarting under the sharp goad of insidious envy': hendiadys.

**338 largus opum** 'a lavish spender'. V. does not intend this as a compliment. For the gen. 'of respect' cf. 416–17.

**339 consiliis ... auctor** 'reckoned no empty authority in council'.

**341 nobilitas:** a technical term, only here in V.: see Introd. 14.

**incertum ... ferebat** 'his paternal ancestry was not known'.

**342 onerat ... atque aggerat iras** 'increases the load of their anger': for *aggerat iras* cf. 4.197; here the metaphor is reinforced by a second verb.

**343–75** Drances' speech. For its length cf. 302–35n. For an analysis see Highet 58–9; Gransden, *VI* 166–7, 177–83. D. supports Latinus' plea for peace, but deliberately provokes Turnus. The eloquence of his speech is not diminished by its motivation.

**343–5** A note of controlled irony marks D.'s opening words: the patronising *o bone rex*, the emphatic *nulli ... nostrae.*

**344 consulis:** picking up Latinus' last words.

**cuncti etc.:** 'The situation is clear to all, it doesn't need any words from me, everyone knows which way the fortunes of our people point, but they hesitate to speak out.'

**345 quid fortuna ferat populi** 'what the destiny of our nation is bringing': i.e. the direction it is taking. Page says that V. 'especially loves to join *ferre* with *fortuna* for the sake of assonance', but an examination of the uses of *fortuna* in the *Aen.* proves that this is not the case: the closest parallel to the present passage appears to be 2.94 *fors si qua tulisset.* More commonly, V. uses with *fortuna* such verbs as *sinere, uetare, uocare, uiam dare,* all of which help the sense of the present passage.

**mussant** 'hesitate': this usage with the infin. appears to be without parallel. The more usual sense, 'hum and haw', 'mutter indecisively', occurs at 454.

**346 det:** sc. Turnus, whose name is suppressed until 363.

**flatusque** 'his full-blown pride' (metaphorical).

**347 ob auspicium infaustum** 'thanks to his ill-starred leadership'. *auspicium* originally meant 'auspices', as at 33: for the extended use cf. 4.102, 7.257.

**moresque sinistros** 'baleful disposition'.

**348 dicam equidem:** emphatic, in antithesis to *dicere mussant* above: '*I* am prepared to say it even if no one else is.'

**349 lumina tot cecidisse ducum** 'so many glorious chiefs have fallen'. The gen. is possessive or perhaps partitive ('from "belonging to" there is an easy transition to "part of"', Palmer 291), the whole phrase constituting a kind of metonymy, the chiefs being defined in terms of their glory. Most commentators compare such common phrases as *lumina ciuitatis, lumina rei publicae*, but these are not strictly parallel.

**351 fugae fidens:** at 10.606–88 Juno had rescued Turnus by sending him in pursuit of a phantom Aeneas, thus taking him out of the front line and back to base: see esp. 10.670 where the baffled Turnus asks *quo feror? unde abii? quae me fuga quemue reducit?* Turnus has not figured in the narrative since that episode, which Drances now exploits for his own ends.

**352–4 unum ... adicias** 'to those gifts which you bid be sent and promised in plenty you should add one more': i.e. Lavinia. *unum etiam* is emphatic, *unum* being repeated in the following line and again elided, as are *te* (354), *natam* (355), *pacem* (356) *ipsum* (358) *horum* (361). *plurima* is predicative, *adicias* is a jussive subjunctive.

**354–5 nec te ullius uiolentia uincat | quin** 'let no man's violence persuade you not to ...' Turnus is again deliberately not named. *uiolentia* is used only three more times in the poem, always of Turnus, at 376, 12.9, 12.45.

**356 des pater** 'give as a father' (predicative). Knauer compares *Il.* 7.350–3, where Antenor proposes to return Helen to the Atridae: 'I see no hope of gain for us unless we do this.'

**357 quod si** 'but if' (cf. 166, 434).

**358 ipsum ... ab ipso** 'the man himself!'

**ueniamque** 'a favour', cf. 101. The tone is one of bitter irony, sustained by *ius proprium* in the next line: T.'s 'right' to Lavinia has been set aside by the oracles (see Introd. 3–4) and, Drances argues, by his own proven unworthiness.

**360** At this point, half-way through this speech, Drances, with powerful effect, begins to address Turnus. Behind the persona of the speaker, the voice of the implied author is unmistakable, especially in v. 362.

**361 caput** 'source': a metaphor from rivers.

**364 inuisum** 'hostile' (cf. Servius, *id est inimicum*). The active sense of this word is rare: see *TLL* s.v. *inuideo* 198.78ff. and cf. Lewis and Short, who cite only two other instances. *OLD* does not distinguish an active sense at all, and Henry, in a long and rather perverse note, argues that the word here bears its normal passive meaning ('hateful') and that Drances is referring to Turnus' feelings towards him rather than his towards Turnus: an interpretation surely ruled out both by common sense and by *infensus* at 336.

**364–5 et esse | nil moror** 'and I don't care if I am'.

**366 pulsus:** see 351n.

**367 et:** postponed; a 'neoteric' mannerism in imitation of Hellenistic usage; Catullus often postpones *atque*, *nec* and *sed*, but never *et*. See Austin's nn. on 2.383 and 4.33, Fordyce on Cat. 23.7.

**367 desolauimus agros** 'we have left our lands deserted': cf. 208–9 *uasti . . . agri*, 8.8. *latos uastant cultoribus agros*.

**369** For the elision of *si* cf. 166n. *adeo* here is to be taken with *cordi est* 'so very dear to your heart'; it more often in V. intensifies the word it follows (275–6n.) but cf. *Ecl.* 2.25 *nec sum adeo informis* 'I am not so very ugly.' Page points out the sneer in D.'s words, which imply that T. cares only for Lavinia's royal dowry.

**cordi est:** this type of elision, really a prodelision or aphaeresis of *est*, occurs quite often at the end of the line.

**371 scilicet:** D. permits himself a final flicker of derision. The sentence *scilicet . . . campis* is more effective if punctuated as a question.

**373–5** For the sentiment cf. *Il.* 3.432–3, where Helen tells Paris to challenge Menelaus face to face (ἐναντίον).

**tu . . . illum:** the pronouns are emphatically contrasted with *nos* ('are *we* to suffer for a cause which concerns only you and T.?').

**patrii . . . Martis** 'your father's warlike spirit': for the personification cf. 389 *Mauors*.

**aspice contra** 'look him in the face': cf. the Homeric phrase ἄντην εἰσιδέειν, *Il.* 19.15.

**375** One of the two incomplete lines in book XI, the other being at 391. Both are effective as they stand. Here the speech ends abruptly at the end of the first foot, as at 8.583, while at 391 Turnus pauses dramatically before his next onslaught. However, there is every reason to suppose that V. intended to complete these *tibicines*: see Gransden, *Aen. VIII* 47–8.

**376 uiolentia:** see 354n.

**377 rumpitque ... uoces** 'and breaks into these words from the depth of his heart': cf. 3.246 *rumpitque hanc pectore uocem* and Williams's n. This highly poetic idiom is first found in V.

**377–444** Turnus' speech takes up Drances' points in order, in the usual rhetorical manner; not until 410 does he turn to Latinus. For an analysis see Introd. 34–5; Highet 59–63, 210–12. Twice as long as Latinus' and Drances', this is the longest and grandest oration in the second half of the poem, if one excludes the story of Hercules and Cacus narrated by Evander in book VIII. It is delivered in scornful and passionate phrases which ring out in the vaunting style of T.'s Homeric predecessors. But Drances' taunt of cowardice rankles deeply: T. refers to it again in his final speech as still needing to be refuted (12.644 *nec Drancis dicta refellam?*).

**378–82** T. rounds angrily on Drances, accusing him of being a 'loudmouth', better at words than deeds. So too did Odysseus round on Thersites, 'fluent orator though you be', for daring to rebuke his betters (*Il.* 2.246). The motif of 'talking rather than fighting' is also Homeric: cf. Nestor, *Il.* 2.342 ('we do our fighting with words only'), Patroclus, *Il.* 16.631 ('it is not for us now to multiply words, but to fight'). See also 460–1.

**379–80 patribusque uocatis | ... curia:** V. uses the Roman technical terms for a meeting of the Senate.

**380–2 sed non replenda ... | agger murorum:** 'But we don't need the senate-house filled with words – your words that fly around so big while you are safe and while the enemy are separated from us by ramparts.' *tibi* may be 'dative of agent' or 'ethic dative': cf. 10.583–4 *uesano talia late | dicta uolant Ligeri.* Both *tuto* and *magna* are predicative.

**383 proinde tona** 'Thunder away, then': for the 'derisive' imperative cf. 460, 738, and for the scansion of *proinde* (disyllabic by synizesis) cf. 400. *meque* and *tu* in 383–4 are bitingly emphatic: '*you* go ahead and accuse *me* of cowardice when your right hand has killed so many ...'

**386 insignis** 'you glorify'; also at 7.790.

**386–7 possit ... licet** 'what quick courage can achieve, you may now discover'.

**scilicet** sustains the irony (cf. 371): 'nor (as you may have noticed) do we have far to look for the enemy'.

**389 Mauors** (archaic form of Mars) picks up Drances' last words. *tibi* is to be taken emphatically with Mauors: 'or will *your* warlike spirit be confined to your windy words and those flying feet?'

**390 uentosa:** again at 708.

**istis:** an ironical emphasis falls on an 'indifferent' word at the line-end; cf. 409 *isto*. For further comment on this line see Introd. 15.

**392 pulsus ego** '*me*, defeated?' (referring back to 366).

**392–5** 'Will anyone charge me with defeat who takes the trouble to look at ... the fall of Evander's house?' *uidebit* is, as Page says, 'a curious future': it has perhaps been influenced by *arguet*. Turnus exaggerates the Trojan defeat, though since Pallas was Evander's only son his house may be said to have been completely flattened. For the remark about the Tiber being swollen with blood cf. the Sibyl's prophecy to Aen. 6.87 *Thybrim multo spumantem sanguine cerno*.

**395 Arcadas:** Greek accus.

**396** 'This was not the experience of me that B. and P. had.' These giant brothers (*ingens* is to be taken with both) were slain by Turnus at 9.672–755, one of his greatest feats of arms. Their Homeric counterparts are Polypoetes and Leonteus, *Il.* 12.127–94; they, however, survived. Turnus' victory over men of such stature is seen as a gigantomachy by Hardie 143–54.

**399 nulla salus bello?** It is normal rhetorical practice to quote an opponent's words back to him in order to refute them or dismiss them with derision: there is another good ex. at 10.25, 10.85. *nulla salus bello* is made to sound like a 'stale old saw' (Page): 'Sing that song to the Trojan chief.' Dido refers to Aen. in the same words at 4.640. Servius points out that by linking Aen. to 'your own fortunes' Turnus covertly accuses Drances of being a traitor; his call for peace will bring comfort to Aen. and advantage to himself.

**400–1 proinde ... | ne cessa** 'carry on, then': T. sarcastically reiterates his own words at 383.

**402 gentis bis uictae:** the same taunt occurs in Numanus' speech, 9.599 *bis capti Phryges*. There are refs. to the earlier sacking of Troy by Hercules at 2.643, 8.157–9, and cf. *Il.* 5.640–2.

**premere** 'disparage': cf. Livy 22.12.12 *premendo ... superiorem sese extollebat*.

**403–5 nunc et ... | nunc et ...** 'in that case [i.e. if your version of things is true] we may suppose further impossibilities: the Myrmidons, Diomedes, Achilles, all terrified of Trojan arms, yes, and the Aufidus flows backwards!' (As who should say, 'Pull the other one.') For the *nunc et ... nunc et* constr. Servius well compares 4.376–80 *nunc augur Apollo, | nunc Lyciae sortes, nunc et Ioue missus ab ipso | interpres diuum fert horrida iussa per auras. | scilicet is superis labor est, ea cura quietos | sollicitat.* In that passage Dido scornfully hurls back at Aen. his claim that divine messages have instructed him to leave her, adding her own ironic comment: 'Of course (*scilicet) that* is what troubles the gods in their quiet calm.' In the present passage, R. D. Williams has argued, *C.P.* 61 (1966) 184–6, that v. 404, which is almost identical with 2.197, should be removed as an interpolation (a view shared only by Hirtzel among modern edd.), on the grounds that Achilles is dead and Diomedes is in fact reluctant to face the Trojans: but this is perhaps to take Turnus' scornful rhetoric too literally. After all, some at least of the Myrmidon chiefs (whose mention in 403 could well have triggered off the poet's recollection of 2.197) might also now be dead. Diomedes is in any case not frightened of the Trojans, but war-weary; his courage in arms has never been in doubt, it is as much a *donnée* of the *Iliad* as the courage of Achilles. Indeed, the mention of Diomedes here perhaps introduces, as Paratore suggests, a note of realism into the catalogue of *adynata*.

**retro fugit Aufidus:** a proverbial figure (the reversal of nature), cf. 8.87, 8.240. The river Aufidus flowed through the territory of Daunus, Turnus' father: cf. Hor. *C.* 3.30.10–12.

**406 uel cum ...** 'or again when he ...' (Page, whose notes here are particularly helpful). In this and the following v., T. again addresses the council; he then addresses Drances for two further vv., 408–9, before turning to Latinus. The ellipse, and the abrupt changes of pronoun, may perhaps be intended to convey the near-incoherence of Turnus' anger.

**407 artificis scelus** 'a schemer's dirty trick'; also of Ulysses, 2.125.

**408 absiste moueri** 'don't run away'; also at 6.399.

**409 isto:** cf. 390 *istis*. With this final flicker of contempt for Drances, T. addresses himself to Latinus.

**411–27** This passage is examined in the Introd. 34.

**411 ultra** 'any longer'.

**415–18** Page points out that this outburst of feeling interrupts the argument begun at 411 and resumed at 419.

**415 quamquam o:** cf. 5.195, where, however, the speaker breaks off immediately. Here the sense is 'But oh, if any part of our traditional courage were still with us, then he would be a noble and lucky man who preferred death rather than such a sight [i.e. the sight of our surrender].' For the motif 'death is better than survival' cf. 159–63, Quinn 14–15.

**416 mihi** 'in my view'.

**416–17 laborum | ... animi:** genitives of respect, cf. 338.

**418** Holodactylic lines are comparatively rare in V. and usually onomatopoeic; cf. 652, 710, 774–5, 875nn. For the phrase 'bit the dust' cf. Homer's ὀδὰξ ἕλεν οὖδας and ὀδὰξ λαζοίατο γαῖαν.

**420 auxilioque** 'for our assistance': predicative dative, cf. 428, 7.551.

**423 tempestas:** for the metaphor cf. 12.284 *tempestas telorum ac ferreus ingruit imber.*

**425–7** 'Many things have the passing days and the shifting labours of unstable time changed for the better; many men has ambivalent Fortune deceived, only to come back to them and replace them on firm ground.' With this resounding generalisation (see further Introd. 34) T. seeks to put fresh heart into the council, and also to reassure himself: there may perhaps be an allusion to his own mysterious restoration to dry land after his pursuit of the phantom Aen., an episode which continues to haunt him (see 351n.). For the expression cf. Ennius, *Ann.* 258–60 *multa dies in bello conficit unus ... | et rursus multae fortunae forte recumbunt: | haudquaquam quemquam semper fortuna secuta est.* Skutsch, however, notes (440–1) that V. has reversed the sense of Ennius' lines, which is that success may be followed by disaster on the same day, a sentiment no commander trying to encourage his men would express. V. is clearly thinking, in any case, not of a single day's reversal but of changing fortune over a long period of time: for *dies* in this sense cf. 5.783.

**rettulit in melius:** cf. 1.281. The sense of *alterna* must be taken with the whole of the rest of sentence, a good ex. of the extended Virgilian constr. discussed at 19–21n.

**428–33** T. here answers the point made by Latinus at 308–9; 'I accept that the Aetolians [sc. Diomedes] will not help us, but . . .'

**429** The repetition of *erit* is, as Williams says, extremely moving and effective. *auxilio* must be understood with both Messapus and Tolumnius. The former is described in the Catalogue at 7.691–2 as the offspring of Neptune and as inviolable by fire or sword; the latter is mentioned again as an augur at 12.258ff. *felixque* may be taken with both; there may well be, as Heyne suggested, an implied contrast with the ill-fortune which dogged Diomedes.

**431 Latio . . . agris:** ablatives after *delectos*.

**432** This is the first mention of Camilla since the Catalogue of Italian leaders (7.803–4).

**433 florentis aere** 'flowering in bronze'; the metaphor is repeated from 7.804, on which Fowler has an interesting note (87–90).

**434 quod si** 'but if': 166n.

**435 tantumque . . . obsto** 'and I am such an impediment to the common good': said with proud and bitter irony.

**436** 'Well, victory has not so spurned in detestation these hands of mine . . .' For *adeo* cf. 369n. *exosa* is predicative.

**437** 'that I should shrink from risking anything when so much is at stake'.

**spe:** either the prospect of saving his people single-handed (Heyne) or his personal hopes of the marriage and the succession (Conington). The former seems the likelier.

**438 animis** 'with courage': cf. 18n.

**uel** (with *ille licet* at 440) 'even though he . . .'

**praestet** 'excel', 'play the role of'. Both meanings are relevant here. There is a strong proleptic irony: at the end of book XII Aen. does indeed assume the role of Achilles.

**439** Both Achilles (*Il.* XVIII) and Aen. (*Aen.* VIII) received armour made for them by Hephaestus/Vulcan. Cf. Turnus' words at 9.148–9 *non armis mihi Volcani . . . | est opus in Teucros.*

**440 ille licet:** the words are emphasised both by their postposition and by the strong sense-break at the second-foot caesura.

**440–2 animam . . . | deuoui** 'I have devoted my life.' Literally, *deuoueo* refers to the religious vow by which a leader offered his own life and that of his enemy to the gods of the underworld, as did the two Decii in 340 and 295 B.C.: see Cic. *Pro Sestio* 48, Livy 8.9.8. At 12.234 Turnus is said by his sister Juturna to have dedicated himself to the gods above (*superos ... quorum se deuouet aris*). Here the formula is extended: T. offers his life to Latinus and his fellow-countrymen.

**440 soceroque** is perhaps a deliberate piece of bravado: so at 9.138 Turnus refers to Lavinia as his *coniunx* as he thinks himself into the role of a second Menelaus.

**442 uocat** refers back to Drances' final words (375): cf. 399n.

**433–4** 'And if the gods *are* angry, let not Drances be the one to appease them with his death, nor, if it's valour and glory, let him be the one to win them.' A resounding final couplet, in which all the emphasis falls on *uirtus et gloria* (see Introd. 34). Cf. the conclusion of Hector's rejoinder to Polydamas, *Il.* 18.305–8.

### 445–497 The war-council breaks up

The council is interrupted by the news that the Trojans are preparing to attack. Cf. *Il.* 2.786–810, in which Iris, disguised as Polites, brings news to the Trojan assembly of a Greek attack, and Hector dissolves the meeting to prepare for battle. See further Introd. 13.

**445–6 Illi ... Aeneas** are in strong antithesis: 'while they were debating ... Aeneas' (Williams).

**448 ecce:** for the dramatic postposition cf. 10.133.

**449–50** The purport of the news is given in *oratio obliqua*: cf. 227–30, 898–900 (also after *nuntius*).

**451 extemplo turbati animi:** also at 8.4. and cf. 618.

**452 stimulis haud mollibus irae:** cf. 728.

**453 manu** 'with outstretched hands': cf. 10.80 *pacem orare manu*. This 'gestural' use of *manu* should be distinguished from its much more frequent appearance in V. with words of action (defend, kill, attack, brandish, etc.) where it adds force and emphasis: cf. 116n.

**trepidi:** cf. 300n.

**454 flent ... patres:** a good example of the flexibility of Virgilian word-order. *maesti* (a key-word of book XI, see Introd. 28) is perhaps best taken adverbially with both verbs: 'the elders lament and mutter gloomily'.

**456 haud secus atque ... cum** 'just as when': cf. 8.243 *non secus ac si* ... For these bird-similes cf. *Il.* 2.459–65. V. also uses swans in another double simile at 7.699–705, where, however, the text may preserve unrevised alternatives (see Fordyce's n.). Here the effect is to provide a moment's breathing-space in the powerful forward thrust of the narrative: cf. the effect of 297–9.

**457 Padusae:** near the mouth of the river Po. The specific local reference is in the learned Alexandrian manner, and contributes to the 'Italian' colouring of the second half of the *Aeneid*.

**458** A strongly onomatopoeic line (*rauci ... loquacia cycni*): *loquacia* ('noisy'), because of the cry of the birds.

**459 immo** 'All right, then' (cf. 9.98, 9.257). The word signals a dramatic outburst and carries an ironic corrective force. T. again expresses his contempt for those who talk about peace while the enemy are attacking (cf. 378–82n.).

**460** For the 'derisive' imperatives cf. 383–4, 401, 738.

**462 sese** is to be taken both with *corripuit*, 'he sprang up', cf. 6.472, and with *extulit*, 'he went out', cf. 12.441.

**464 equitem** 'the cavalry'.

**464–5 Messapus ... Coras:** nominatives for vocatives. For Messapus see 429n., for Coras and Catillus see 519n.

**465 latis ... campis** 'widely over the plains'; *latis* is predicative, cf. 8.8 *latos uastant cultoribus agros.*

**467 iusso:** archaic future perf., cf. 9.154 *faxo.*

**468 discurritur** 'they were running' (impersonal passive).

**469 pater:** for the 'lengthening' of the second syllable cf. 111, 323nn.

**470** The alliterative symmetry of this slow, spondaic line (*d*, *t*, *t*, *t*, *d*), enclosed in two verbs signifying weakness and despondency, conveys the now complete isolation of Latinus, whose powerlessness to control events has already been described at 7.594–600.

**differt** 'adjourns'.

**471 qui non acceperit** 'for not having accepted': causal subjunctive. Latinus did in fact at first accept Aeneas as his destined son-in-law (7.268–73) but subsequently weakened in his resolve through the violence of Turnus' opposition. In his speech to the council he made no mention of his daughter, and even suggested that the Trojans might be willing to leave the country.

**ultro** 'of his own accord'. V. has this 'indifferent word' at the end of the line 15 times in the *Aeneid*, but only four times in the first five books:

an instance of the growing flexibility of his technique as the writing of the poem proceeded.

**473 praefodiunt** 'dig trenches in front of'.

**475 corona** 'cordon': also at 9.508, 10.122, 12.744.

**477–85** The women of Latium, led by queen Amata, proceed to the temple of Athene and pray to the goddess, as their Trojan counterparts had done in the *Iliad* (6.297–310), that the spear of their deadliest foe might be broken. This foe is Aeneas, as for the Trojans it was Diomedes, so that Aeneas now assumes the role of Diomedes, who has just removed himself from the present conflict. The Homeric scene was depicted on the murals in Juno's temple at Carthage, 1.479–81: *interea ad templum non aequae Palladis ibant | crinibus Iliades passis peplumque ferebant | suppliciter, tristes et tunsae pectora palmis.* See further Introd. 16, Gransden, *VI* 184.

**477 nec non:** an emphatic transitional formula introduced into poetry by V.: also at 603, 6.183, 8.646, 9.169, 10.27, 12.23. More usual is *nec non et:* see Fordyce on 7.521.

**-que** is epexegetic: *Palladis* must be taken in common with both *templum* and *arces.* The temple is on the citadel like its Homeric counterpart, νηὸν ... Ἀθήνης ἐν πόλει ἄκρηι (the temple of Athene on the Acropolis).

**478 subuehitur** 'rides'. V. may have thought of Roman matrons' right to ride in upholstered carriages (*pilenta*): see Gransden on 8.665–6.

**magna ... caterua:** the abl. is 'instrumental-sociative' (Palmer 300–1, Hofmann–Szantyr 115). Austin points out (n. on 1.312) that the instrumental abl. normally replaces *ab* with abl. of agent after *comitatus, stipatus,* etc., and some such nominative participle agreeing with *regina* may be understood here; V. might also have been thinking of a participle agreeing with *caterua* (*stipante, urgente,* etc.) as at 564, 1.497, 2.40, 2.370, 4.136, where the abl is an abl. absolute.

**479–80** Lavinia is the *causa mali tanti* prophesied by the Sibyl to Aen. at 6.93. For the hiatus *tanti, oculos,* cf. 5.735, 10.136, 10.141; there are altogether nine such instances in the poem.

**oculos ... decoros:** cf. 35n.

**482 maestas:** a key-word of book XI (Introd. 28) in a solemn spondaic line.

**483–5** The three-line prayer is closely modelled on *Il.* 6.305–7: 'Lady Athene, protectress of the city, shining among goddesses, break the spear of Diomedes, and grant also that he himself fall prone in front of the Scaean Gates.' For *armipotens* cf. 2.425. and for Pallas' role as protectress of citadels (Homer's ῥυσίπτολι, *Il.* 6.305) cf. 2.615, where she is also referred to as *Tritonia*: for this obscure cult-title see Austin on 2.171 (it apparently refers to a lake or river near which the goddess was supposed to have been born). *praeses* usually refers to the tutelary guardianship of a place; here the goddess is said to preside over war itself.

**484 praedonis** 'pirate', also used of Aen. by Amata, 7.362, and by Mezentius, 10.774. The word chimes effectively with *praeses*, a contrast of meanings pointed by the alliteration of *pr* reinforced with *pronum* (Homer's πρηνέα) in the following line.

**486-97** The arming of Turnus: cf. 12.81-102, where he is compared to a bull.

**487 adeo:** cf. 275-6n.

**thoraca indutus:** cf. 35n.

**488-90 auro | ... aureus:** for T.'s golden glitter cf. 9.269-70 *quo Turnus equo, quibus ibat in armis | aureus,* 12.87-8 *ipse ... auro squalentem ... | circumdat loricam umeris.*

**491 animis et spe:** see 18n.

**492-7** For this simile cf. *Il.* 6.506-11 (= 15.263-8), the arming of Paris and Hector: see Schlunk 25-30. The simile was first rendered into Latin by Ennius, *Ann.* 535-9 *et tum sicut equus qui de praesepibus fertus | uincla suis magnis animis abrumpit et inde | fert sese campi per caerula laetaque prata | celso pectore; saepe iubam quassat simul altam, | spiritus ex anima calida spumas agit albas.* For a comparison between V.'s treatment of the simile and its Homeric and Ennian models see Skutsch 683-5, Williams, *TORP* 695-6, 732-3, and cf. also D. West, 'Multiple correspondence similes in the *Aeneid*', *J.R.S.* 59 (1969) 47.

**493 potitus** 'having reached': cf. 1.172.

**494** For this deictic use of *ille* to draw special attention to the subject cf. 7.787, 9.796, 10.274; it is usually resumptive, as here, but sometimes anticipatory, as at 809 below.

**496-7 alte** should probably be taken both with the preceding words and with *luxurians*: see G. B. Townend, 'Punctuation in the Latin hexameter', *C.Q.* N.S. 19 (1969) 341-2.

### 498-531 Turnus and Camilla prepare for battle

**498 Obuia cui:** cf. 10.380 *obuius huic; obuia* is repeated below, 504.
**501 ad terram defluxit:** *OLD* compares Furius Bibaculus 8 (9)

*habenas* | *misit equi lapsusque in humum defluxit*, Livy 2.20.3 *moribundus Romanus ad terram defluxit*; but these passages describe an involuntary fall, while V. presents a graceful, sweeping act of dismounting. See also Wigodsky 100.

**502–6** The first of Camilla's three brief speeches. She speaks again during her *aristeia* over a conquered foe, in the Homeric manner (715–17) and finally at her death (823–7).

**502 sui ... forti** 'if the brave with good cause feel some confidence in themselves'; *sui* goes with *fiducia*. C. is talking about herself, as the next line shows, but, as Williams points out, *fiducia* is a quality which would commend itself to T. (cf. 9.126, 10.276).

**503 promitto** usually takes the accusative (of the person promising) with the future infin., but the plain present infin. is found in Plautus and is here helped by attraction to the constr. with *audeo*. The double elision of *-o* is very striking and is unparalleled elsewhere in the *Aen*. The only other elision of *-o* at the end of a first person singular verb with a cretic pattern ($- \cup -$) in the *Aen*. is at 1.391 *nuntio*; but such elisions were doubtless helped by the tendency to shorten the final *-o* in spoken Latin: this is reflected in V.'s scansion of *nescio* as a dactyl in several passages in the *Eclogues* and *Georgics* and at *Aen*. 2.735, and cf. also *scio* at 3.602.

**504 contra:** another 'indifferent word' placed emphatically at the end of the line (cf. 282). For the anastrophe of prepositions cf. 282, 510.

**505 manu:** cf. 116n.

**507 oculos ... fixus:** cf. 35n.

**horrenda** 'awe-inspiring'; also used of the Sibyl at 6.10, and of Juno at 7.323.

**509–10 sed ... supra** 'but since that courage of yours is all-surpassing'. An effective dislocation of word-order, with another 'indifferent word' (*quando*) postponed to the end of the line (cf. 201n.); for the anastrophe of *supra* cf. 282, 504. *iste* is not here ironical, merely emphatic (contrast 390).

**partire:** imperative.

**511–13** Turnus' military strategy is carefully planned but is abandoned as a result of Camilla's death (896–915). The narrow pass in which he hopes to ambush Aen. resembles the Caudine Forks, where a Roman army was trapped by, and surrendered to, the Samnite general Gavius Pontius, 321 B.C.: see Livy 9.2–6. Aeneas had better luck.

**512 improbus** is predicative ('has had the nerve to'). V. uses this adj. seven times in the *Aen.*: all but one of its occurrences are in the last four books. Two meanings may be distinguished: (1) pejorative, as here, when a speaker wishes to slight an opponent: cf. 5.397 *improbus ille* 'that damned fellow', 12.261 *improbus aduena* 'that damned newcomer'; (2) with the sense 'uncontrollable', 'relentless', used by the narrator of an implacable foe, as at 767 below (Camilla), 9.62 (a wolf), 12.250 (an eagle), 12.687 (a mountain, = Homer's ἀναιδής).

**513 quaterent** 'with orders to harass' (jussive subj.), cf. 1.645. Virgil, like other poets, often dispenses with purely grammatical signifiers like *ut*, and makes the verbs do the work: the aim is, in the words of Marouzeau (211), 'moins de mots que de sens'; ellipse, asyndeton, parataxis, are all means to this end.

For the metaphor, cf. 9.608 *quatit oppida bello*, and the Ennian formula at 875 (n.).

**515 furta paro belli** 'I am preparing an ambush.'

**516 biuias** 'at both ends'.

**517** 'You engage and take the enemy cavalry.' *signa conferre* is the normal Latin for 'engage in battle'.

**excipe** 'catch': a hunting metaphor, appropriate to C.: cf. 3.332, *Ecl.* 3.17–18.

**518** For Messapus see 429n.

**519 ducis ... curam** 'you also take on the role of joint commander' (with Turnus, not with Messapus, who will be subordinate to C.).

**Tiburtique manus:** Tiburtus and his brothers Catillus and Coras were said to have founded Tibur. The latter are compared in the Catalogue of Italian leaders to Centaurs (7.675), thereby emphasising their primitive power and their horsemanship: see Fowler 52–4, Heinze 197.

**522 Est:** the usual signal for a topographical ecphrasis: see 316n.

**ualles:** old form of the nominative, cf. 7.565.

**523–9** The distinctive features of this landscape – a wooded valley surrounded by a range of hills with only one way in and one way out, by way of two defiles linked by a single track crossing a central plateau – occur also in Livy 9.2.7–9: *saltus duo alti angusti siluosique sunt montibus circa perpetuis inter se iuncti; iacet inter eos satis patens clausus in medio campus herbidus aquosusque, per quem medium iter est; sed antequam uenias ad eum, intrandae primae angustiae sunt, et aut eadem qua te insinuaueris retro uia repetenda aut, si ire porro pergas, per alium saltum artiorem impeditioremque,* *euadendum.* 'Two deep defiles, narrow and wooded, are joined by a range of mountains on either side; shut in between them lies a quite extensive plateau, grassy and well-watered, with the track running through the middle, but before you reach it, you must enter the first defile and either leave by the way you came or, if you want to go on, leave by the other defile, which is even narrower and less easily passable.' See further N. Horsfall, 'Allusion and reality in Latin topographical writing', *G.&R.* 33 (1985) 200–1, where it is argued that such descriptions are typical rather than specific, and that the writer is drawing on epideictic rhetoric rather than a precise knowledge of the actual location. In Virgil's version, the words *densis ... latus* also occur at 7.565–6, where there is a similar ecphrasis describing Amsanctus.

**523–5 quam ... maligni** 'closed in on both sides, dark with dense undergrowth; a narrow path leads there, confined entrances with awkward access form the approach'. A characteristic double 'theme and variation': *ferunt* ('lead') repeats the sense of *ducit* while *-que ... -que* are epexegetic, as also at 526–7.

**526–7** 'Above this valley, on high ground on the hill-tops, is level ground, hidden and providing safe shelter.' The meaning is that troops could be stationed on this plateau who would be invisible to the enemy trapped in the valley below.

**528–9** 'whether you chose to attack from left or right, or to take your stand on the ridge and rain down missiles'.

**530 huc:** the normal signal that the ecphrasis is finished: cf. 8.423, 8.606.

**regione** 'direction': see Austin on 2.737.

**531 iniquis** 'unfavourable' (to the enemy): cf. 525 *maligni*. For this military usage see *OLD* s.v. 6b with exx. from the historians.

### 532–96 The story of Camilla

See also Introd. 20–2.

A brief transition leads into Diana's speech to her nymph Opis, in which she laments Camilla's impending fate, tells the story of her early life, and instructs Opis to take vengeance on the man destined to kill her. Camilla's story is a kind of aetiological ecphrasis. Arrigoni (66) sees it as an explanation of Camilla's tomb (mentioned at 594), but there is no independent evidence for the existence of such a monument. Evan-

der's long aetiological narrative of the fight between Hercules and
Cacus in book VIII, explaining the rite at the Great Altar of Hercules,
is somewhat different, since that cult was in actual existence at Rome.
Evander's speech and Diana's do, however, offer a similar formal
structure, in that both lead into an exhortation: *quare age* (Evander),
*uerum age* (Diana). Diana's speech can be seen aetiologically, in that it
explains the goddess's abiding affection for Camilla: the key lines here
are 537–8, in which the statements *cara mihi ante alias. neque enim nouus
iste Dianae | uenit amor* are explained in the ecphrasis that follows. (For
another ex. of the 'tale within a tale' giving the reader informatioi
relevant to the immediate narrative, cf. Venus' disquisition to Aeneas
about Dido, 1.335–71.)

The speech presents some difficulties. Diana refers to herself three
times in the third person. The first of these self-references, at 537 (quoted
above) is awkward, coming as it does in the same verse in which she
has referred to herself as *mihi*, but it might be justified, as also might the
third reference, *sola contenta Diana* (582), as emphasising the pathos of
the words: Heinze (416n. 2) compares Amata's words at 12.56 *per si
quis Amatae | tangit honos animum.* The second self-reference, *donum Triuiae*,
adds an antiquarian touch which seems as inappropriate to a goddess
as does the learned etymological information at 543, though such details
can be readily paralleled in authorial discourse elsewhere in the poem,
e.g. 5.117–23. Evander's disquisition also includes such information,
but he is a local antiquary and an obvious 'voice' of the poet himself.
The suggestion that these third-person references represent quotations
from Camilla or Metabus seems unlikely: see M. Bonfanti, *Punto di vista
e modi della narrazione nell'Eneide* (Pisa 1985) 189 n. 23.

Mackail and other commentators have observed that the entire
passage from 537 *neque enim* to 584 *intemerata colit* is detachable, and that
*uellem* at 584 resumes the narrative of present events broken off at 537.
This observation has suggested to some the hypothesis that Virgil
originally wrote the ecphrasis as a separate piece of authorial narrative,
which he then fitted into its present place (see Heinze 416n. 4). If so,
it was an inspired piece of adaptation, for the passage gains most of its
pathos from its context: a flashback to Camilla's early years as her life
approaches its end. It is highly unlikely that the episode was ever
intended for insertion into the description of Camilla in the 'Catalogue'
at the end of book VII, a suggestion decisively rejected by Fowler 90 n.

1 (cf. Schweitzer 35, Klingner 585–6), but revived by Williams, *TIA* 285. There are inconsistencies in the two passages. Diana implies that Camilla is going to war for the first time, but in VII she is said to be inured to battle: *non ... colo calathisue Mineruae | femineas adsueta manus, sed proelia uirgo | dura pati ...* (7.805–6); and she is presented as the anti-type of the idealised stay-at-home Roman matron, *adsueta colo calathisue Mineruae*, depicted at 8.408–10. Nor is her role as huntress and votary of Diana referred to in VII (see Introd. 22–4). But such difficulties merely serve to remind us of the poem's unrevised state. (Further comments may be found in Büchner 396; Arrigoni 17n. 8, 33n. 48; Paratore on 11.532; *EV* I 629 s.v. 'Camilla').

**532 interea** marks a change of subject and location: cf. 12.791 *Iunonem interea rex omnipotentis Olympi ...*; there too the syntax is similar, the reader being directed first to the new object (in the accus. case) and after that to the new subject. On V's mastery of narrative transition see Gransden, *VI* 46–51.

**Opim:** accus. of Opis, a nymph of Diana who came from Thrace (cf. 858) to Delos.

**534 tristis:** with *uoces*.

**Latonia:** Diana, daughter of Leto.

**537 cara mihi:** repeated at 586.

**537–8 iste ... amor** 'nor is that love [of mine] a recent phenomenon'. Page translates *iste* 'that love you know so well', but *iste* does not always carry a second-person reference: cf. 2.708 *iste labor*, which Austin transl. 'that burden you make', but which might mean simply 'such a burden'. In both passages *iste* emphasises something just expressed by the speaker.

**538 -que** (=*nec*): disjunctive, cf. 592.

**dulcedine:** a Lucretian word for 'love of kind', only here in the *Aen.*, but cf. *Georg.* 1.412, 4.55.

**540** Privernum was the last stronghold of Volscian resistance to Rome in 329 B.C. (Livy 8.19–21), but its link with Metabus and Camilla is not attested before Virgil. It is not clear exactly why Metabus was expelled (for *pulsus ob inuidiam* at 539 cf. the parallel expulsion of Mezentius, of whom the same phrase is used, 10.852), or under what circumstances Camilla returned to lead the Volscians. See further Arrigoni 66–8, *Enea nel Lazio* (the official catalogue of the Virgilian bimillenary exhibition, Rome 1981) 78–9.

The elision of *cum* in the fourth foot of the hexameter is rare: cf. 7.528, 10.503, 12.941.

**542 exsilio:** predicative dat., to be taken with *comitem*: 'a companion for his exile'.

**543** As a *doctus poeta* V. frequently displays an interest in names and their origins: cf. the etymology of Latium given by Evander at 8.322–3. On the name Camilla see further Introd. 24–5.

**545 solorum:** used of places, as we say 'the lonely woods'. Cf. 569.

**546 milite** 'soldiery': collective singular, cf. 600.

**547 ecce** often signals a dramatic development in the narrative. It is especially frequent in book II: see Austin's n. on 2.57, 2.203, and cf. Gransden, 'The fall of Troy', *G.&R.* 32 (1985) 63, 72.

**547–9** 'Suddenly, they being in mid-flight, the river Amasenus overflowed and foamed on the top of its banks, so great a downpour had burst from the clouds.' *tantus ... ruperat* explains the previous sentence: the constr. is paratactic, cf. 513n. In prose the clauses would be reversed, and *tantus imber se ruperat* would be followed by *ut*.

**550 caroque oneri timet** 'fears for his precious burden'.

**550–1 omnia ... sedit** 'as he turned over every possibility he came reluctantly to this sudden decision' (Williams). *subito uix* is an effective oxymoron: M. is desperate and needs to make a quick decision, yet the only course open to him is one he accepts reluctantly, for it is a gamble with his daughter's life.

**552–4 telum ... quod forte gerebat | ... | huic:** the sentence is an anacoluthon; *telum* has no verb to govern it, but is picked up by *huic*. The effect is to throw the noun into prominence before the construction of the main clause has taken shape: 'luckily, being a warrior, he was carrying his huge spear, and to this he tied his daughter ...' For the constr. see Conway on 1.573.

**553 bellator** is predicative.

**solidum ... cocto** 'a solid piece of knotted and seasoned oak' (hendiadys).

**554 libro ... subere** 'cork bark from the woods' (another hendiadys).

**555 habilem** is predicative: 'tied her neatly to the middle of the spear'. According to Servius, the critic Probus (first century A.D.) described this incident as 'an unconvincing invention' (ἀπίθανον πλάσμα). However, the use of cork in crossing rivers crops up again in Plutarch,

*Pyrrhus* 2.3–7 (a message is written on bark and tied to a stone, which is then thrown across a river: see Arrigoni 89 n. 203); and in Plutarch's *Life* of Camillus (25), P. Cominius used cork to swim across the Tiber. But the touch of fairy-tale fantasy in Virgil's story is exactly right for Camilla: here perhaps for the first time we see her safely skimming the waters as she seemed to do in her mature womanhood, see 7.810–11 *uel mare per medium fluctu suspensa tumenti | ferret iter celeris nec tingeret aequore plantas.*

**556 ita ad aethera fatur:** also at 10.459. There are no other instances in V. of the elision of *ita.*

**557–60** Before casting the spear, Metabus prays to Diana and dedicates his daughter to her service. For the prayer before discharging a weapon cf. 9.404–9, where Nisus also prays to Diana, *nemorum Latonia custos,* and cf. also *Od.* 24.520–3, where Athene tells Odysseus to pray to her and to Zeus before casting his spear at Eupeithes.

**558–9 tua … fugit:** almost a metaphysical conceit: 'the first weapon the baby "holds" is yours, goddess, it is as your suppliant that she flees through the air from the foe'. M. dedicates both weapon and child at 566.

**562–3** Effective onomatopoeia. The break at *immittit* marks the throwing of the spear, while the enjambment and the unusual rhythm at the end of 562 (cf. 143, 170nn.) contribute to the effect. For *sonuere* cf. 7.701 *sonat amnis.*

**564** For the elision of *iam* cf. 846n., 900, Austin on 2.254, Soubiran 405–18.

**566 donum Triuiae** 'an offering to Diana'. Triuia (Gk τριοδῖτις, 'of the crossroads') is an epithet of the chthonic deity Hecate, who had become identified with Artemis: like other attributes of Artemis it was transferred to the Italian wood-spirit Diana when the two were assimilated.

**568 neque … dedisset** 'nor, in his wild state, would he have consented' (i.e. to the restrictions of civilisation). *feritate* is a good ex. of V.'s flexible use of the ablative 'with a widely concomitant force' (Mackail 513): cf. 8.256 *animis* 'in his fury'.

**569 pastorum … aeuum** 'a shepherd's life'.

**571–2** 'He brought up [his daughter] on wild milk from the teats of a brood mare, milking its udders into her tender lips'.

**armentalis:** '*quae inter armenta feturae causa pascatur*' (Servius).

**mammis et lacte ferino:** hendiadys.

**573–4 utque ... | institerat** 'and when the infant had planted footprints with her earliest feet', i.e. as soon as she had taken her first tottering steps. *pedum* may be taken both with *uestigia* (cf. 7.689–90) and with *plantis* (cf. 8.458) in a kind of ἀπὸ κοινοῦ construction.

**576** 'No gold head-band for her, no long cloak to cover her, but instead ...'

**577** The tiger-skin seems to have covered her head as well as her back (though *a uertice* could simply mean 'down'): cf. 680, 7.667, where animal skins do cover the warrior's head. But the detail is not here significant: V. is merely saying that C. lacked the ornaments and fine dress of a noble maid, and had only a tiger-skin to cover and adorn her.

**578 iam tum** 'already'.

**579 tereti** 'smooth'.

**circum caput egit habena:** also at 9.587. For the sling as the hunter's weapon cf. *Georg.* 1.309, where the word for the thong or strap is *uerber*, not *habena*.

**580 Strymoniamque:** another ex. of the ornamental local epithet or 'poetic geography' in the learned Alexandrian manner (cf. 457,773). The cranes of the Strymon river in Thrace were famous: cf. 10.265, *Georg.* 1.120.

**deiecit** 'brought down', cf. 5.542.

**581–2** An allusion to Catullus 64.42 *multi illum pueri, multae optauere puellae* (see n. on 68–71). Here the delayed verb is anticipated by *frustra*, a figure noted by Servius.

**582–4** 'Content with Diana alone, she fosters her perpetual love of hunting and virginity, herself inviolate.' The strikingly symmetrical v. 583, with its enclosing word-order and assonance of *-orum ... -orem*, is 'framed' inside the two participial adjectives *contenta ... intemerata*: the effect is to emphasise C.'s self-contained and sequestered life.

**584 uellem** marks the return to the discourse interrupted at 537: see above, 532–97n. *uellem ... fuisset*: 'I could have wished she had not been caught up ...'; *uellem* is past potential, *fuisset* a past unfulfilled wish; the constr. of the two verbs is paratactic, cf. 513n.

**585 tali:** military service, rather than the service of Diana.

**586** 'And would she were now one of my dear companions' (literally, 'would she were dear to me and ...'): the expression must be read as a hendiadys, for C. still is *cara* to Diana (see 537) but is no longer one of her companions, having abandoned her pastoral life.

**587 uerum age:** marking an exhortation to action after a digression, like *quare agite* at 8.273 (cf. 532–97n.). The remainder of Diana's speech falls into two parts. The goddess instructs Opis to kill Camilla's slayer, whoever he may turn out to be, and herself undertakes to convey her body to its burial place. These are the limits of her power over fate. Opis carries out her orders at 836–67. The divine protection of a slain hero's body is a Homeric motif: V. alludes here specifically to *Il.* 16.667–83, where Zeus sends Apollo to convey Sarpedon's body to its burial place. The parallel is close, for Zeus did not save Sarpedon, dear to him though he was: cf. also Schlunk 14–16. The reader may also recall the death of Dido, at the end of book IV: Juno could not save her, but sent Iris to ease her passage to death.

**592 -que** 'or'.

**593–4** Cf. *Il.* 16.453–7, 16.667–75.

**595–6** Opis descends to earth. Knauer compares the passage of Iris to Olympus, *Il.* 8.409–10. For *delapsa* of a divine descent cf. 7.620 (Juno), and for the whole picture cf. the descent of the Fury at 12.853–5 *harum unam celerem demisit ab aethere summo | Iuppiter inque omen Iuturnae occurrere iussit: | illa uolat celerique ad terram turbine fertur.*

### 597–647 The cavalry engagement

**597 At:** V.'s favourite signal for a major narrative transition, here reinforced by the equally common *interea* (cf. 1n.). For the two together cf. 10.689, 12.383–4.

**599 numero** 'by number'.

**600 sonipes:** collective singular, cf. 464 *equitem*, 546 *milite*. The word was first used in epic by V., followed by all his successors: see Austin's n. on 4.135.

**601–2** The fields sprout spears: a striking metaphor, of which a more explicit version, using *seges* instead of *ager*, is at 7.526, 12.663. Here the transferred epithet *ferreus* makes the point. *horrere* is used of anything that stands up spikily: cf. 8.654 (the bristling thatch of the *casa Romuli*).

**603 nec non:** see 477n.

**604** For Coras and his brother see 519n.

**605–6 hastasque ... dextris:** the lances were long, so that even with the right hand drawn back (ready to throw) the weapons might be said to stretch forward a long way. For *reductis dextris* cf. 5.478–9 *reducta | ... dextra.*

**607 ardescit** 'increases in intensity': to be taken with both subjects.

**609 furentisque:** the line is a hypermetric hexameter, the final syllable being elided into the following line. V. uses these twenty-one times, all but three of the instances being with *-que* or *-ue*. Hypermetre is rare in earlier Latin hexameters and the only Greek ex. is in the first hexameter of an elegiac epigram of Callimachus, 41 Pf. For further details see Fordyce on 7.160. No special effect seems intended here, with the enjambment running smoothly, but contrast 4.629, the most famous ex. in the *Aeneid* of hypermetre.

**611 ritu** 'in the manner of': for the simile cf. *Il.* 12.156.

**caelumque ... umbra:** cf. 12.578 *obumbrant aethera telis.*

**614–15** Strikingly onomatopoeic vv., with a marked alliterative and assonantal pattern : *p, qu, qu, p, p, p, dant, -dantum.* For *quadripedantum* ('gallopers') cf. 8.596 *quadripedante putrem sonitu quatit ungula campum.* Polysyllabic words occur rarely at the end of a line in V., though freely admitted by Lucretius and Catullus: cf. 6.483, 12.363, where, however, the vv. are an imitation of Homer, *Il.* 17.216. These exx. represent the only five-syllabled endings in the *Aen.:* quadrisyllabic endings are less unusual, e.g. 69 *hyacinthi,* 355 *hymenaeis,* 4.215 *comitatu;* at 659 below (n.) *Thermodontis,* the fifth foot is a spondee.

**615–17** 'Like a thunderbolt or a weight hurled by a siege-engine, Aconteus is thrown, and falls far away [from his horse] ...' The imagery is violent and cosmic: Hardie (178 n.61) notes a 'latent storm-comparison running through the episode, starting with 611 *niuis ritu*'.

**praecipitat:** intransitive, as at 2.9.

**618–19 uersique ... uertunt:** in his n. on 7.491 Fordyce includes this among exx. of V.'s 'non-significant' repetitions. But in poetry it could be said that all repetitions, word-play, 'figurae etymologicae', etc., are significant (cf. Introd. 28). Here the past participle passive and the active verb enact between them, through enclosing word-order, the rout of the Latins and their ride for safety to the walls. *uersi* is picked up again at 629 *uersos.*

**reiciunt parmas:** they slung their shields over their shoulders to cover their backs during their retreat.

**621 iamque propinquabant portis** 'and now they were on the point of approaching the gate'; also (with *propinquabam*) at 2.730, and cf. 6.358 *iam tuta tenebam,* 8.657 *tenebant:* the so-called 'imperfect *de instanti*' of an action left incomplete.

**622 colla:** sc. *equorum*, cf. *Georg.* 3.204.

**623 hi:** the Trojans.

**624–8** A splendid simile, not really Homeric (Heyne compares *Il.* 11.305–8, to which Knauer adds *Il.* 14.16–19, but neither is really parallel). V.'s precise and accurate word-picture of waves advancing and retreating (624 *alterno ... gurgite*) on a rocky beach has an Alexandrian accuracy of observation. For a finely observed account of the action of waves by an English poet see G. M. Hopkins's *Journal* for 13 August 1874, edd. H. House and G. Storey (Oxford 1959) 215: 'Heavy seas: we walked along the sea wall to watch them. The wave breaks in this order: the crest of the barrel "doubling" is broken into a bush of foam ... a lace and tangle of jumping sprays; then breaking down these grow into a sort of shaggy quilt tumbling up the beach; thirdly this unfolds into a sheet of clear foam and running forward in leaves and laps the wave reaches its greatest height upon the shore ... after that, raking on the shingle ... it is forked and torn and ... these rents widen; they spread and mix and the water clears and escapes to the sea transparent and keeping in the end nothing of its white except long dribble bubble strings which trace its set and flow.'

**625 superiacit** 'smashes over': a rare word.

**625–9** The onrush and retreat of the waves is presented in two pairs of brilliantly onomatopoeic lines: *nunc ruit ad terram* is balanced by *nunc rapidus retro*, and there is a marked alliterative pattern of *r* and *s*.

**630 terga tegentes:** alliterative word-play.

**632 legitque uirum uir** 'each marks his man'; V. was perhaps thinking of *Il.* 15.328 ἔνθα δ' ἀνὴρ ἕλεν ἄνδρα ('there man killed man'). For the rhythm of the line-ending cf. 10.361, 10.734 *uiro uir*; such endings generate a conflict of metrical ictus and stress; there are more than 30 exx. in V. This particular ending is first recorded in a line of the poet Furius Bibaculus, preserved by Macrobius 6.3.5 *pressatur pede pes, mucro mucrone, uirum uir*. See further Conington on 10.361, Fordyce on 7.592.

**633–5** The writing here is highly stylised and hyperbolic, with the conventional epithet *alto* and the epic doubling of *-que*, here yielding another unusual rhythm and forming part of a chain of copulatives. The repetition of *uirorum* after *uirum uir* emphasises the heroic force of the passage and prepares the reader for the naming of particular heroes.

**636–45** There is no good reason to follow Mackail in regarding these

vv. as spurious. M. argued that without them *pugna aspera surgit* would
continue and be completed in vv. 646–7, but in fact the mention of
blood at 646 would follow too soon after *sanguine in alto*, whereas if the
passage is retained, vv. 646–7 will represent a return to, and summary
of, the general account of the carnage. This would be entirely in V.'s
manner. Nor is there anything in the text itself to arouse suspicion: for
*ipsum horrebat adire* (636) cf. 5.378–9 *nec quisquam ex agmine tanto | audet
adire uirum*, and for the wounding of the horses cf. 10.888–94.

**636** Orchilochus' death at the hands of Camilla is described at
694–8.

**641 ingentemque ... ingentem:** cf. 171n.

**corpore et armis:** cf. 4.11 *pectore et armis. armis* is a well-known
ambiguity, but here (and Austin and Henry argue that the same applies
to 4.11) it seems clear that the word is from *armus*, 'shoulder'. V. is here
referring to physical strength, as is clear from 643–4. Herminius scorns
armour, relying on his strength alone.

**643–4** It seems best to punctuate lightly, since the sense is unbroken:
Herminius' shoulders are unprotected and he does not fear wounds, so
massively does he confront Catillus' weapons.

**645 duplicatque ... dolore** 'and the spear driven through him
doubles up the hero in pain'; a striking phrase.

**transfixa:** of the spear, not, as commonly, of that which it pierces.

**646 funditur ... cruor:** the rhythm is unusual (three dactyls in
which metrical ictus and accent coincide, and with no strong caesura
until the fourth foot). The effect is onomatopoeic: blood flows freely in
the mêlée.

**647 pulchramque ... mortem:** V. first used this motif in *Georg.*
4.218 (identical wording), then of Nisus, 9.401 (*properet* for *petunt*).
*pulcher* is a moral not an aesthetic signifier: see Arrigoni 57; L. Alfonsi,
'Pulchra mors', *Latomus* 22 (1963) 85–6, with references to Soph. *Ant.*
72, 96.

## 648–867 *Aristeia* and death of Camilla

See Introd. 21–5.

**648** A strikingly dramatic line, introduced by V.'s favourite transitional conjunction *at* (cf. 597).

**exsultat Amazon** 'prances like an Amazon'. Camilla's self-transformation from *uenatrix* to *bellatrix* is here completed. There may be a reference here to the variant reading of the last line of the Iliad, ἦλθε δ' Ἀμάζων, 'and then came the Amazon', inserted to introduce Penthesilea (see 661 below). Arrigoni (34) sees an allusion to Homer's πολυσκαρθμοῖο Μυρίνης, 'war-dancing Myrina', *Il.* 2.814; *exsultare* is used of the Amazons again at 663, and of Turnus at 491, just before he is compared to a horse.

**649 unum ... pugnae** 'with one breast exposed to the battle'. The right breast was traditionally exposed (perhaps originally mutilated). Cf. the description of Asbyte in Sil. Ital. *Pun.* 2.56–88, clearly modelled on V.'s Camilla, where it is stated that the right breast was exposed; cf. also Penthesilea in Quintus Smyrnaeus 1.594. The artistic evidence is indecisive: sometimes one breast is shown exposed, sometimes the other: see D. von Böthmer, *Amazons in Greek art* (1957), esp. pl. lxxxix. In Roman art, the striking though late (third-cent. A.D.) sarcophagus of Achilles and Penthesilea shows a number of Amazons, some with the left breast exposed, some with the right: see R. Strong, *Roman imperial sculpture* (1961) pl. 120. A good and easily accessible selection of illustrations can be found in Tilly, and cf. also H. Sichtermann and G. Koch, *Griechische Mythen auf römischen Sarkophagen* (Tübingen 1975) pls. 21–8.

**650 manu:** cf. 453n.

**denset** 'causes to come thick and fast'. The verb also occurs in the first conjugation, Enn. *Ann.* 267 *densantur campis horrentia tela uirorum.*

**652** The holodactylic line, with its marked correspondence of ictus and accent, resounds and echoes onomatopoeically.

**aureus** is to be taken with both *arcus* and *arma*.

**654 fugientia:** transferred epithet; it is Camilla who is here retreating and firing arrows behind her in the manner of the Parthian light cavalry, cf. *Georg.* 3.31 *fidentemque fuga Parthum uersisque sagittis.*

**655 at circum lectae comites** 'Yes, and around her [rode] her chosen comrades ...' The three names are strongly Italian, the last two indeed strongly Roman: 'Larina' is connected with the Samnian town of Larinum, 'Tulla' suggests the early Roman king Tullus, 'Tarpeia' the vestal virgin after whom the Tarpeian rock was said to have got its name.

**657 Italides:** apparently a Virgilian coinage, borrowed by Statius.

**dia:** this Ennian and Lucretian form of *diua* is used by V. only here: the unique usage, following on the old Roman names, emphasises V.'s vision of Camilla as the heroic and spiritual incarnation of archaic Italy.

**657–8** '... whom she had chosen to be an ornament to herself and worthy attendants in peace and war'. *quas ... delegit* varies *lectae* above; *decus* and *ministras* are predicative.

These vv. offer further homage to the women of archaic Italy. Dante saw in Limbo Camilla, Penthesilea and Lavinia, together with Lucretia, Marcia wife of Cato of Utica, and Cornelia mother of the Gracchi (*Inferno* 4.124–8).

**659–63** This simile completes the identification of C. and her companions with the Amazons and acts as an extended epiphonema to the paragraph which began at 648: a good ex. of ring-composition. There is irony in these allusions, for Hippolyte was defeated by Hercules, Penthesilea slain by Achilles.

**659 quales:** a common compression in similes ( = *tales fuerunt quales*): see Conway on 1.430–1. Hexameters ending in a quadrisyllable with a spondee in the fifth foot were a hallmark of the Alexandrians and of the Roman 'neoteric' style: there are 30 exx. in 408 vv. in Catullus 64, whereas V. in over 12,000 hexameters has only 33 instances, usually with Greek proper names, though not always (e.g. 8.167 *intertextam*).

**660 pulsant** 'make to echo': cf. 7.701–2 *sonat amnis et Asia longe | pulsa palus*. This refers to the noise of hoof-beats along the river-bank: it is less likely that V. intends the reader to think of the noise made by hoof-beats on frozen water (see Henry's n.).

**pictis ... armis** probably refers to shields (cf. *picti scuta* at 7.796), perhaps decorated with gold and silver: see Fordyce on 8.588 and cf. 12.281.

**Amazones:** scanned as a Greek word with a short final syllable.

**661** 'Perhaps with Hippolyte, or when warlike Penthesilea rides back ...'

**663 exsultant:** see 648n. If, as Arrigoni (47) thinks, the reference is to a victory dance on horseback, the allusion is tragically ironical, for Camilla herself will never ride back in triumph.

**lunatis:** for the crescent shields cf. 1.493, where Penthesilea is depicted on the murals in Juno's temple at Carthage.

**664** The apostrophe focuses attention on Camilla and recalls

Homer's address to the doomed Patroclus, *Il.* 16.692–3: 'Then who was it you slaughtered first, who was the last, Patroclus, as the god called you to your death?'

**666–9** 'One of the most horrible death scenes in the *Aen.*' (Quinn 349: an interesting discussion).

**666 Clytio ... patre** 'whose father was Clytius' (abl. absolute).

**667 aduersi** 'as he came at her'.

**transuerberat** 'pierced'; also at 10.336, 10.484.

**abiete** is scanned as a dactyl, the *i* being consonantal, cf. 890, Fordyce on 7.175.

**668 atque:** for the use of this word unelided in the fifth foot see 183n. and cf. 725. Here, however, it does not link the two parts of a formulaic phrase, but enables the sense to flow over into the following line: so too at 12.332–3 *increpat atque furentis | bella mouens immittit equos.*

**669 suo se in uulnere uersat:** a highly effective ex. of enclosing word-order; for the elision of *se*, cf. 632, 815.

**670 super** 'on top [of him]'. A verb must continue to be supplied for the accusative nouns from 664–5.

**671 suffuso:** this seems to be the reading preferred by Servius, though he also registers the variant *suffosso*. He explains the former as referring to a condition of the feet which causes stumbling, to which Conington objected that a lame horse would not have been brought into battle: but the word need only mean that the horse went lame, stumbled and was about to fall ('*casuro*', Servius). *suffosso* would mean 'stabbed underneath', which would not redound much to C.'s glory.

**670–2 quorum ... inermem** 'of these two the former [was killed] while recovering the reins after falling from his horse as it stumbled under him, while the latter [was killed] as he came to Liris' help and stretched out his weaponless hand to his fallen comrade'.

**672 subit:** cf. 10.338.

**674 incumbens eminus** 'attacking from a distance': cf. 10.645 *instat cui Turnus stridentemque eminus hastam | conicit.*

**677 Phrygii:** the narrator's sympathies seem strongly pro-Italian here; the word is used dismissively of the Trojans by the Italians, e.g. 484.

**678 ignotis** 'unfamiliar'.

**679–81** 'who, when he became a fighter [as distinct from a hunter, *uenator*], had his shoulders covered with a skin stripped from a bullock and his head with the huge gaping mouth and jaws of a wolf with their white teeth'.

**681 cum dentibus albis:** cf. 7.667, where Aventinus, son of Hercules, is depicted wearing a lion's head complete with teeth: see Fowler 47–9.

**682 sparus:** a kind of hunting-spear or javelin. All these accoutrements suggest a pastoral figure turned warrior.

**682–3 cateruis | uertitur ... uertice:** a marked pattern of assonances.

**684** 'She took him in the retreat and thrust him through (without much trouble).' It seems best to follow Mackail's punctuation here, placing *neque enim labor* in parentheses: as he says, 'what made it easy for C. to bring down Ornytus was not the fact that her opponents were in retreat, but that he wore no defensive armour' – the point emphasised throughout vv. 677–89.

**685 super ... fatur:** repeated from 10.556 (Aeneas' taunt over Tarquitus). *super* is adverbial.

**686 siluis** is emphatic: C. herself was *siluestris*, but she has become a true soldier, not least in her own eyes.

**687–8 aduenit ... redargueret** 'the day has come for a woman's arms to refute your words'. The intricate interlacing word-order emphasises the two verbs which begin and end the sentence.

**redargueret:** the imperfect subjunctive is read by all MSS and is normal syntax: see E. J. Kenney, *J.R.S.* 60 (1970) 260, citing several Virgilian parallels, e.g. *Ecl.* 9.47–8 *ecce Dionaei processit Caesaris astrum,* | *astrum quo segetes gauderent frugibus et quo* | *duceret ...*; *Georg.* 2.350–2 *iamque reperti* | *qui saxo super atque ingentis pondere testae* | *urgerent.*

**688 nomen** 'glory'.

**689 hoc** is emphatic: 'still, this glory at least you shall take home with you'. Cf. Aeneas' words to Lausus, 10.829 *hoc tamen infelix miseram solabere mortem:* | *Aeneae magni dextra cadis.*

**690 Orsilochum et Buten:** the constr. continues the series of accusative nouns, C.'s victims, begun at 666 and picked up at 670 (*primum ... tum ... protinus*).

**691** The force of *sed* derives from *maxima ...* | *corpora*: massive men, but she found Butes' weak spot and then went after Orsilochus with her battle-axe (*securim* = *bipennem*, 651). For the death-blow dealt to

Butes cf. Achilles against Hector, *Il.* 22.322–7, and for the slaying of Orsilochus cf. Achilles against Demoleon, *Il.* 20.397–400 (motif of braining) and the immediately following death of Hippodamas (killed trying to run away).

**auersum** 'with his back turned', in contrast to Orsilochus, who gives chase until himself pursued. Following the pattern of a Homeric *aristeia*, V. makes C. irresistible (cf. the use of *auertere* in 703) until the moment of her downfall. The reading of the old edd. was *aduersum* (cf. Dryden: 'But Butes breast to breast . . .'), vigorously defended by Henry.

**692–3** The liquid alliterative pattern of these two vv. provides a momentary lightening in the harsh and violent onrush of this passage.

**693 lucent** 'was visible': cf. 144, 9.383.

**laeuo ... lacerto:** his shield was hanging slack, not in the on-guard position.

**694–5** C. dodges O., who is pursuing her in a large circle, by doubling back inside the circle, so that the pursuer becomes the pursued.

**696 perque ... perque:** more epic doubling of *-que*.

**698 congeminat:** used of the redoubling of blows (with magnificent word-play) at 12.713–14 *dat gemitum tellus; tum crebros ensibus ictus | congeminant, fors et uirtus miscetur in unum.* Here the axe is repeatedly and horribly brought down.

**700–1** The Ligures, who lived in the northern Apennines, had a reputation for trickery (Conington compares Cic. *Pro Cluentio* 26.72): see 716 below. We are not told the name of this son of Aunus: Servius assumes it was Aunus too, though v. 717 suggests otherwise. The four-word hexameter (700) is first found in Hesiod and is frequent in Apollonius; it is relatively uncommon and effective in V. (23 instances in *Aen.*): cf. 870n.

**702 se ... euadere pugnae** 'to get himself clear from the battle': *OLD* gives no other instances of *euadere* with the dative, but the constr. with the reflexive verb is similar to that normally found with verbs like *eripere, subducere* (cf. 10.50, 10.615).

**704** 'He began to ponder a trick with cunning guile.' *consilio ... et astu* is a kind of hendiadys, reinforcing the sense of *dolos. ingredior* with the infin. is a common prose constr.

**705 tam** is elided only twice in the *Aen.*, here and at 1.568: see Norden Anh. xi 2.

**707 te** must be supplied with *accinge*.

**708** 'You'll soon find out to which of us vain boasting will bring harm.'

**gloria** 'love of fame', but also 'vanity': cf. Hor. *C.* 1.18.15 *et tollens uacuum plus nimio Gloria uerticem.*

**fraudem:** again at 717, where it must be translated 'deceit'; Page and Williams so render the word here, but 'harm' is the likelier meaning. Servius translates the word as *poenam* ('penalty', 'unpleasant result'); he also records, but rejects, an alternative reading *laudem* (preferred by Henry, who compares 791–2 below).

**709 dolore** 'anger', resentment'.

**710** The holodactylic line well conveys C.'s swift response to the Ligurian's taunt.

**711** Her shield was unemblazoned because she had not previously been in combat (cf. 9.548), in contrast to the Amazons described at 660. (For the inconsistency between this line and 7.805–6 see Comm. on 532–97 above.)

**interrita** emphasises the courage of the virgin warrior, who now faces her opponent on foot.

**712 uicisse:** *se* must be supplied, as at 8.534.

**717 fraus:** cf. 708.

**Auno:** the more usual constr. with compounds of *fero* is with *in* or *ad* (cf. 10.668 *et patris antiquam Dauni defertur ad urbem*), but the 'dative of motion towards' is not uncommon with compound verbs, e.g. 5.34 *et tandem laeti notae aduertuntur harenae.*

**718 ignea** 'like fire': cf. 746. C. outruns her opponent's horse: for her swiftness of foot (a characteristic she shares with Homer's Achilles) see 7.807, Introd. 22.

**719–20 aduersa ... | congreditur** 'meets him face to face' (predicative).

**721–4** She kills Aunus' son as easily as a hawk disembowelling a dove. The gory details of the Ligurian's death are implied in the simile, which in effect takes over the narrative. Cf. *Il.* 22.139–40, where Achilles in pursuit of Hector is compared to a hawk pursuing a dove, but there the dove continually eludes the hawk; at *Od.* 15.526–7 (not a simile) a hawk holds a dove in its talons and plucks its feathers, but there is no blood and no disembowelling. See also 751–4n.

**721 sacer:** Homer called the hawk 'swift messenger of Apollo' (*Od.* 15.526). Servius says the bird was sacred to Mars, and also suggests that

V. might have been playing on the Greek word for 'hawk', ἵρηξ, which resembles ἱερός ('sacred').

**725–67** Tarchon rallies the Etruscans. For this Etruscan king, the friendly counterpart of the 'bad' Etruscan Mezentius, see Gransden on 8.506. In accordance with an oracle which ordered the Etruscans to seek a foreign-born leader to oppose Mezentius, Tarchon offered the post to the Greek Evander, who, however, declined on the grounds of age and passed it to Aeneas: see further 8.497–513.

**725–8** This is the only appearance of Jupiter in book XI. Cf. 10.689–90 *at Iouis interea monitis Mezentius ardens | succedit pugnae*; the present passage is more fully anthropomorphic, making use of several Homeric motifs: the god looks down with watchful eyes (*non … nullis … oculis*) on the battlefield (cf. *Il.* 8.51); the god affects a hero directly (cf. *Il.* 11.543, 15.592); the god inspires a hero to rally his followers (cf. *Il.* 8.217–19, in which Hera arouses Agamemnon). See further Williams, *TIA* 21–35.

**725 hominum sator atque deorum:** also at 1.254. The phrase is a variant of Ennius' *diuum pater atque hominum rex*, used by V. at 1.65 (see Austin's n.), 10.2. For *atque* see 183n.

**725–6 non … nullis … oculis** 'with watchful eyes': litotes, as pointed out by Servius. There is another ex. at 728 (*haud mollibus*).

**728 stimulis … iras:** cf. 452.

**inicit** 'instils': often of feelings, though not elsewhere in the *Aen.* Heinsius' emendation *incutit* would yield a further echo of Ennius, *Ann.* 533 (*incutit iram*): cf. *Aen.* 1.69 *incute uim*, with Servius' n.; Putnam 207.

**729 caedes cedentiaque:** Latin, and indeed most poetry, is fond of this kind of word-play.

**731** 'Calling each man by his name': as Agamemnon instructs Menelaus to do when rallying the Achaeans at *Il.* 10.68.

**732–40** For Tarchon's taunts cf. those of Agamemnon, *Il.* 4.338–48.

**732 o numquam dolituri** 'O you who will never feel shame'.

**733 quae … uenit?** 'What great cowardice is this which has invaded your hearts?' For the idiom cf. 1.606 *qui tanti talem genuere parentes?*

**734** There seems no good reason to break the run of three rhetorical questions with which T. begins his outburst (the O.C.T. prints an exclamation mark at the end of this line).

**palantis:** sc. *uos.*

**haec** is emphatic: 'ranks as strong as ours are' (Conington).

**735 quo** 'to what purpose': for the ellipse cf. Hor. *Ep.* 1.5.12 *quo mihi fortunam, si non conceditur uti?* For the sentiment cf. *Il.* 21.474.

**736-8** 'But, no laggards when it comes to love and nocturnal riots, or when the curved flute has announced some Bacchic dances, then sit and wait for the feast ...' Williams and the O.C.T. place a full stop after *Bacchi*, which means that *estis* must be supplied with *segnes*, but this would make *exspectate* too abrupt. For the 'derisive' imperative (read by most MSS and by Servius) cf. 460, 9.617, 9.620. The reading *exspectare*, adopted by Page and Conington, has little authority, but would make good sense: for the explanatory or epexegetic infin. (with *segnes*) cf. Hor. *C.* 3.21.22 *segnesque ... soluere.*

**739-40** Marked onomatopoeia, with a preponderance of dactyls (correspondence of ictus and accent in the second half of each line) and repeated echoes of *u* (*um, um, -undus*, *harus*pex, *nun*tiet): the effect is of ease and languor, the antithesis of martial alertness, and the tone is sarcastic: 'this is what you love, this is what you fancy ...'

**secundus** 'propitiously': the adjective is predicative, having been, as it were, transferred from the omens (the *sacra*) to the soothsayer.

**741 moriturus et ipse** 'ready himself also to die'.

**742 turbidus** 'frantically', 'violently' (predicative). The word is connected with *turba* = 'disorder', 'confusion', and keeps this sense at 814 below; it may also be connected with *turbo* = 'whirlwind', cf. 10.603-4, where Aeneas is said to be *turbinis atri | more furens*.

**745 tollitur in caelum clamor** is an Ennian phrase (*Ann.* 428).

**746 uolat igneus aequore Tarchon:** the dactylic rhythm, and the correspondence of ictus and accent, convey the effortless speed of T.'s advance.

**igneus:** see 718.

**aequore** 'over the plain' (locative ablative).

**747 arma uirumque** 'the man and his weapons': recalling the opening words of the poem. The phrase became a cliché: see Austin on 1.1.

**750 sustinet** 'holds off'.

**dextram:** i.e. his enemy's.

**uim uiribus:** 'figura etymologica', cf. 632 *uirum uir.*

**exit** 'eludes': cf. 5.438 and similar transitive use of *euadere.*

**751-4** Another bird-simile, showing some resemblance to the previous one (721-4): there the hawk showed the dove no mercy, here the eagle shows none to the snake. Cf. *Il.* 12.200–9 (a descriptive passage, not a simile), in which an eagle lets go of a snake, which falls to the ground in front of Hector and Polydamas: the latter interprets the omen as a sign from Zeus that they should not attack the Greek ships, but Hector dismisses the omen. In his adaptation V. links the simile closely with the narrative, for Tarchon does not let go of Venulus, nor did Camilla let go of the Ligurian (721–2n.). This is characteristic of Virgilian similes, which intensify and advance the narrative as well as being poetic display-pieces.

These lines offer a strikingly onomatopoeic alliterative pattern: *s, s, s, u, u, squ, squ, s, s*. Some of the phrasing resembles that at 5.273–9, another snake-simile, cf. especially *sibila colla | arduus attollens* with *sibilat ore | arduus insurgens*. V. is fond of snake-imagery but does not describe snakes from life, but from literary sources: their scales do not 'stand up'.

**755 arduus insurgens:** V. frequently uses *arduus* adverbially with a present participle in asyndeton: for other examples see Gransden on 8.299.

**757 Tiburtum:** gen. plural; the men of Tibur (on the Anio, 18 miles N.E. of Rome, the modern Tivoli) were fighting with their joint chiefs and co-founders: 64on.

**758 ducis exemplum ... secuti** 'following the successful example of their leader' (hendiadys).

**759 Maeonidae:** the Etruscans, who were supposed to have come from Maeonia in Lydia.

**fatis debitus Arruns:** A. kills Camilla but is doomed by Diana (see 590–2).

**760–1 uelocem ... circuit** 'circles round swift Camilla, leading her on with much cunning spear-work'.

**iaculo et multa ... arte:** hendiadys.

**prior:** he 'makes the running', 'keeps one step ahead'. The word-order is intricately interlaced as pursuer and pursued draw closer together.

**762–5 qua ... hac ... qua ... hac:** the carefully balanced lines imitate the way in which the movements of Camilla and Arruns correspond.

**766–7** The rounding-off couplet which concludes this eight-line passage depicts Arruns prowling ceaselessly round C. trying to find his opportunity. The lines are highly onomatopoeic, with the repetition of

*hos aditus* and the interlacing alliteration of *d, qu, d, qu, c, c, c, qu.* Cf.
5.441–2 (depicting a boxer trying to get a blow home) *nunc hos, nunc
illos aditus, omnemque pererrat | arte locum.*

**improbus:** 512n.

**768–77** An ecphrasis describing Chloreus' gorgeous apparel, in appropriately ornate diction: see Introd. 23. Gold is associated elsewhere
in the *Aeneid* with 'barbarians' (i.e. non-Italians, which included the
Trojans prior to their assimilation): see the description of the Gauls at
8.659–61.

**768 Cybelo:** Cybelus was the mountain of the goddess Cybele and
is here used, as Servius says, *pro numine*; this reading should be preferred
to the more obvious *Cybelae* ('difficilior lectio potior'): cf. 3.111.

**770–1 quem ... tegebat** 'which was covered with a cloth of bronze
scales joined together with gold to form a plume'. It appears that the
horsecloth was covered with brazen scales buckled together with gold
clasps, so that the horse was effectively armoured. Servius quotes Sallust, *Hist.* 4.65 *equis paria operimenta erant, quae linteo ferreis laminis in modum
plumae adnexuerant* (*linteum* = Virgil's *pellis*). Soldiers who rode armoured
horses were called 'catafracti' or 'cataphracti', cf. Livy 35.48.3 *equites
loricatos, quos cataphractos uocant.*

**in plumam:** Servius compares *Aen.* 6.42 *excisum Euboicae latus ingens
rupis in antrum* 'to form a cave.' Cf. also 776 *in nodum.*

**772 ferrugine** 'dark purple': the foreign (for *peregrina* cf. 777 *barbara*)
cinnabar dye from Spain: see Mackail on 6.303 and cf. 9.582 *pictus acu
chlamydem et ferrugine clarus Hibera.*

**773** Both epithets are of the type found at 580 (n.). Lycia and the
Cretan town of Gortyna were associated with bows (cf. 4.70, 8.166).

**774** Cf. 8.659 *aurea caesaries ollis atque aurea uestis.*

**774–5** Two consecutive holodactylic lines add sonority to the ornate
and exotic description. The passage is further distinguished by alliteration of *c* and *qu* and by the use of foreign words: *cassida*, 'a plumed
helmet' (=*cassis*), may be Etruscan (see *OLD*); *croceus, chlamys* and
*carbasus* are all Greek.

**775–7** 'Then he had fastened his saffron tunic with its rustling folds
of linen into a knot with a yellow gold [sc. buckle or brooch] and his
tunic and outlandish trousers were decorated with embroidery'.

**chlamydemque sinusque:** hendiadys. For the unusual postposition of the first *-que* cf. *Georg.* 2.119.

**tunicas ... tegmina:** for the accusatives see 35n.

**778 templis:** perhaps of Diana (Arrigoni 52–3), though it is usually hunting trophies which are dedicated to her, not military ones (e.g. 9.406–7). Camilla's (or the implied author's) uncertainty as to her intention with regard to Chloreus' gear may perhaps illustrate her ambivalent role: see further Introd. 23, and cf. Williams, *TIA* 117: 'the poet enters the text to condemn her'. In marked contrast is Aeneas' brisk despatch of the priest Haimonides, *totus conlucens ueste atque insignibus albis*, at 10.537–42. On the proper disposal of *spolia* see further R. O. A. M. Lyne, 'Virgil and the politics of war', *C.Q.* n.s. 33 (1983) 193–203. Chloreus is finally killed by Turnus, 12.363.

**779–80 captiuo ... | uenatrix** 'or whether with the object of flaunting herself in captured gold when she went hunting'. For *captiuo* cf. 2.765 *captiuo auro*, 7.184 *captiui currus*; the adj. is common in prose but is not found in this sense in verse before V.

**783–4** A striking ex. of Virgil's handling of narrative. We left Arruns at 765–7, prowling, circling, biding his time, with Camilla his prey. Then at 768 the focus shifts to Chloreus, who becomes the subject of an ecphrasis, until he in turn slips away from the centre of the reader's vision into the accusative case, and Camilla (*uirgo*, cf. 762) becomes the subject, the pursuer; and now, in these two vv., there is another dramatic shift. First we see a spear, *telum* – whose? Then at *cum tandem tempore capto*, with the emphatic effect of a spondaic word filling the fourth foot, we have a sudden awareness of crisis, and Arruns, placed emphatically after the caesura, becomes the agent of the narrative, and, in due course, Camilla's slayer.

**784 concitat et ... precatur** 'threw, praying as he did so'. The two actions are simultaneous, the more immediate one being placed first, the second appended by parataxis rather than subordination. For this idiom, see also Austin on 2.353, Gransden on 8.85.

**785–93** Cf. the famous prayer of Achilles to Zeus, *Il.* 16.233–48, for the success and safe return of Patroclus: see Introd. 19. There are also exx. in the *Iliad* of Trojan heroes praying to Apollo, e.g. Pandarus at 4.119 (reported as indirect speech), Glaucus at 16.514. Arruns' prayer (and here the parallel with Achilles is at its closest) is partly successful, partly not.

**785–8** The Etruscan Arruns is presented by Virgil, who frequently works antiquarian lore into the *Aeneid*, as a priest of Apollo Soranus, a local deity worshipped at Soracte (modern Soratte), the isolated mountain 26 miles north of Rome (celebrated by Horace, *C.* 1.9). These priests were called Hirpi (from the Etruscan word for wolf, cf. the Roman Luperci) and practised fire-walking (cf. Plin. *N.H.* 7.19). Their origin would have been apotropaic: Servius tells how wolves carried off the *exta* from the fire and were pursued by the priests to the wolves' cave, whence a lethal pestilence was emitted (it was thought unlucky to pursue a wolf: see Coleman on *Eclogues* 9.54). The priests ended the pestilence by 'becoming' wolves: at 809–11 Arruns is compared to a wolf. Arruns' reference to Camilla as *pestis* (792) is a nice touch.

**786 quem primi colimus** 'whom anciently we serve'; or perhaps (with Conington, supported by Williams) 'whose chief worshippers are we'.

**786–7 cui ... | pascitur** 'in whose honour the blazing pine-heap [literally 'the pine-blaze from the heap'] is fed'. See Mackail's Appendix A on V.'s uses of the ablative.

**788 multa ... pruna** 'deep in the live ashes'.

**790 omnipotens** carries great emphasis as the last word of the sentence and the first word of the line.

**791–2 laudem | facta ferent:** the normal assumption about an epic hero's deeds of prowess, cf. 8.287–8 *carmine laudes | Herculeas et facta ferunt.* Arruns says he will let his other deeds take care of his glory: as for the killing of C., this is a military necessity and so long as (*dum*) it is achieved he is content to go home *inglorius* (as indeed he does: the adj. carries a proleptic irony).

**794–804** See further Introd. 19, 24.

**795 mente dedit** 'willed': cf. 10.629.

**partem ... in auras:** this formula for words spoken in vain (cf. 798) is not used by Homer of Achilles' prayer for Patroclus. *Il.* 16.250, but cf. *Od.* 8.409 (a wish that any words of ill omen may be carried away by the winds). In Latin cf. Cat. 30.9–10 *omnia ... uentos irrita ferre,* 64.142 *cuncta ... discerpunt irrita uenti, Aen.* 9.312–13 *aurae | omnia discerpunt et nubibus inrita donant.*

**798 inque Notos** is pleonastic and virtually = *in se:* for a note on this idiom see E. J. Kenney on *Moretum* 61 (Bristol Classical Press 1984).

**799 ergo ut** 'and so when'. For the noise of the weapon rushing through the air cf. 863.

**800 animos** 'attention': cf. 12.251 and Conway on 1.149. *acris* 'keenly': predicative adj. to be taken in common with both nouns.

**801–2 nihil...nec...memor** 'she was totally unaware of' (supply *erat*); for *nec ... nec ... aut* cf. 12.135 and 280n. on *-ue*.

**803–4** On the violence and sexual imagery of these powerful lines see P. Heuze, *L'Image du corps dans l'œuvre de Virgile* (Ecole française de Rome 1985) 175, 333–4. For the wound in the right breast cf. Aphrodite in *Il.* 5.393, Penthesilea in Quintus Smyrnaeus 1.594. The lines are given further emphasis by the assonance and enclosing word-order of *hasta ... haesit*. For the emphatic position of *haesit* cf. 790 *omnipotens* and see Introd. 21 on V.'s placing of 'sense-breaks' early in the line.

**806–8** For the flight of Arruns cf. the flight of Euphorbus after hitting Patroclus, *Il.* 16.812–15 ('... and lost himself in the crowd, not enduring to face Patroclus ...'), and also the flight of Antilochus at *Il.* 15.585–6; the latter also carries a simile: see below, 809–11n.

**807 laetitia mixtoque metu:** cf. 3.99–100 *mixtoque ingens exorta tumultu | laetitia*, 10.871 (= 12.667) *mixtoque insania luctu*. *mixto* is attached to one noun but applies to both. For the elision of *iam* see 564, 846nn.

**809–11 ille ... lupus** 'like that wolf': *ille* is deictic, cf. 494n., 9.63 (another wolf-simile), 10.707 (boar-simile), 12.5 (lion-simile). On the present simile see further Williams, *TIA* 175–7. For Arruns' wolf-connections see 785n. The structural model for Arruns' flight is to be found in Homer's Euphorbus, who runs away after wounding Patroclus (*Il.* 16.813), but for the simile cf. Antilochus (*Il.* 15.585–6) 'who did not hold his ground, but fled away like an animal which has done something bad'.

**prius quam ... sequantur** 'before hostile darts can pursue ...': the subjunctive reflects unfulfilled purpose or intention.

**810 auius abdidit altos:** the rhythm, here emphasised by alliteration, is onomatopoeic, reflecting the ease with which Arruns slipped 'out of the way' (for *auius* cf. 12.480). Cf. 814, where *abdidit* is picked up in *abstulit*.

**812–13 caudamque ... utero** 'and drooping his tail he tucks it in panic between his legs' (Williams). *remulceo* is a very rare word, not cited by *OLD* before V. and in V. only here.

**pauitantem:** a boldly transferred predicative adj. (=*pauitans*).

**814 turbidus:** see 742n.

**816–17** Carefully constructed verses: the alliterative pattern *m* and *t*, the postponed connective *sed* (cf. Austin on 6.28), the very expressive bucolic diaeresis (cf. Gransden on 8.198) and the placing of an 'indifferent' word at the end of the line (cf. 201, 374, 390, 409, 471, 504,

509, 824, 873) are all devices which engage the reader's special attention, while there is a powerful sense of finality in 817, secured by the
enclosing word-order and the symmetrical disposition of nouns and
adjectives – the mechanism, so to speak, of C.'s death – around the
emphatic monosyllabic verb *stat*.

**manu:** cf. 453n.

**818 labitur ... labuntur:** the anaphora serves, as often, both as a
connective device and for emphasis. It also carries the alliteration of *l*
into the following line.

**frigida:** of the cold of death; again at 828, cf. 4.385, 12.951, Lucr.
3.390.

**819 purpureus quondam color** 'the glowing colour she once had':
for *purpureus* of the bloom of youth cf. 1.590–1 *lumen ... iuuentae |
purpureum*, and the colour of the flower in the simile which accompanies
the description of Euryalus' death, 9.435.

**821–2 fida ... curas** 'faithful to Camilla above all others and the
only one with whom she shared her troubles'; *Camillae* is dative, *quicum*
is archaic, *qui* being the old abl. of all genders; *partiri* is the infin. of
repeated or characteristic action, see Austin on 4.422: only here in
V. in a subordinate clause.

**823 soror:** so addressed by C. as a member of her 'sisterhood' (see
820).

**823–7** Camilla's touchingly brief last words may be compared with
the self-vaunting last speech of Turnus to his sister, 12.632–49. He
thinks only of justifying himself, and of the taunts of Drances; Camilla
thinks only of cause for which she has fought.

**829 exsoluit se corpore:** cf. 4.703 *teque isto corpore soluo*.

**830 relinquens:** for the present participle cf. 828 *fluens*. For the
reading *reliquit* cf. 819, 845 (also with 'variae lectiones'). Servius also
mentions another reading, *relinquunt* (i.e. the arms fall from the hands
of the dying C.).

**831** = 12.952, the last line of the poem. See Introd. 10 and cf. also
the death of Lausus, 10.819–20 *tum uita per auras | concessit maesta ad Manis
corpusque reliquit*.

**832–5** After the intense emotional climax of the previous passage,
these lines serve as a transition to the final scenes of the book.

**832–3 ferit aurea clamor | sidera:** cf. 2.488 *ferit aurea sidera clamor*,
on which Austin well comments: 'the epithet is not otiose, for it marks

the contrast between the patines of bright gold in the serene heavens, and the horror upon earth; so at Camilla's death (11.832)'.

**834–5 densi:** an ex. of the so-called 'constructio ad sensum': a masculine adj. qualifying the compound subject *copia ... duces ... alae*, since they are in fact all men.

**836–7** The death of Arruns: Opis carries out Diana's instructions (see 590–2). The interval in the narrative between commission and execution seems to have been modelled on Apollonius' narrative of Aphrodite's sending of Eros to wound Medea, *Arg.* 3.151–3, 275–84: see W. Kuhn, *Götterszenen bei Vergil* (Heidelberg 1970) 64, 150–2.

**836 Triuiae:** see 566n.

**839 mulcatam** 'worsted', 'beaten up' (by death). There appears to be no recorded parallel for this metaphorical use of *mulcare*, a word which is normally used in such phrases as *mulcare quemquam usque ad mortem*, etc. (see *OLD*). One MS reads *multatam* ('punished by death'), cf. Cic. *De orat.* 1.194 *uitia hominum ... morte multantur*, a sense which might be confirmed by *crudele luisti | supplicium* immediately below. Either word might suggest the other to the implied reader, and all poets exploit such lexical ambiguities.

**841–8** These vv. spoken by Opis constitute a brief, moving funeral oration, compared by Cartault and Arrigoni (62n. 133) to Evander's funeral speech for Pallas, 152–81.

**841 heu nimium** is not found before V., and in the *Aen.* only here, 4.657 and 6.189: see Clausen 150n. 83.

**843 desertae** 'in solitude' (predicative).

**845–7** The sentence is a characteristically constructed tricolon: theme and two variations, each colon being a double negative (*non ... in-, neque ... sine, aut ... in-*): for *aut = neque* cf. 12.135 *tum neque nomen erat nec honos aut gloria monti*.

**846 iam:** for elision of this monosyllable cf. 564n. According to Austin (on 2.254) V. generally restricts this usage to phrases in which *iam* is either preceded or followed by a monosyllable (564 and 8.557 constitute exceptions). For the present phrase, which also occurs at 2.447, Austin compares Cat. 76.18 *extremam iam ipsa in morte tulistis opem*, where *iam* is again elided.

**847 aut famam patieris inultae** 'nor shall you suffer the report of being unavenged'.

**848–9** Opis echoes the words of Diana at 591–2.

**849–51** A brief topographical ecphrasis describes the barrow of king Dercennus of the Laurentes, of whom nothing seems to be known; *hic* at 852 ( = 'here') signals the return of the narrative.

**ingens ... bustum:** enclosing word-order.

**851** The unusual rhythm of this line is due to the 'false ending' created by the correspondence of ictus and accent not only in the last two feet, which is common enough, but in the third and fourth feet also. Such vv. are rare in the *Aen.*; other exx. are at 8.453 and 8.549. All these vv. have a strong caesura in the 2nd foot and a bacchius ($\cup - -$) before the diaeresis at the end of the 4th foot; in the present v. there is also a weak elision of *que* and a marked alliterative pattern of *qu, c.*

**852–3 hic ... sistit** 'here the goddess in all her beauty with a rapid swoop first stationed herself'; *primum*: her first act, before she kills Arruns.

**854 uana tumentem** 'emptily exulting'; *uana* is an adverbial accus.: for a list of similar expressions in the *Aen.* see Page on 9.632 *horrendum stridens* 'whirring horribly'. For the symmetry of this line, and the rhyming participles, cf. 4.260 *Aenean fundantem arces et tecta nouantem.* In both these exx. the elision prevents a full 'leonine' hexameter; 865 below has a similar structure.

**855–6** An echo of Achilles' words to Hector, *Il.* 20.429: 'Come nearer, so that you may the sooner reach your appointed doom.'

**855** is a variation on 5.162 *quo tantum mihi dexter abis? huc derige cursum.*

**857 tune ... Dianae?** '[and to think that] *you* are to die from the weapons of a goddess!' Opis means that Arruns does not merit such a distinction. The words are spoken, Servius observed, with great bitterness.

**858–62** V. is here indebted to Apollonius' description of Eros shooting at Medea, *Arg.* 3.280–5.

**858–9 aurata ... pharetra:** enclosing word-order.

**infensa** 'with deadly intent'; the adj. is often used adverbially, cf. 5.587.

**860–1 donec ... capita:** marked alliteration; the whole passage is in V.'s grandest manner. *capita* = 'the ends of the bow'.

**manibus ... aequis:** this is explained and amplified in the following lines, in V.'s usual manner. Opis' hands were in perfectly balanced tension at the moment of firing, the bow taking the maximum strain, her left hand guiding the arrow-head, her right hand and the bowstring touching her breast.

**862 laeua:** elision of a long vowel before a short one is not uncommon in the first foot of the line but is rare elsewhere; when it does occur in the first foot it is usually of *i* or *o*, cf. 3.315 *uiuo equidem*, 3.623 *uidi egomet*; there appears to be no other instance in V. of the elision of a long *a* before a short one; the effect in speaking the line would be to 'lose' the short *a* of *aciem*.

**863** Another description of the arrow 'singing' in flight, cf. 799–801.

**866** Arruns' brief moment of prowess is over; he is already forgotten; Diana's revenge is complete.

**867** An epiphonema, or rounding-off line. Opis, her mission accomplished, returns to Olympus. Though not technically 'golden', the line, with its regular symmetry, absence of elision and careful disposition of assonance and alliteration, restores a sense of calm and order before we return to the confusion of the battlefield.

## 868–915 Epilogue

The Rutuli are thrown into disorder by Camilla's death. Turnus abandons his plan to ambush Aeneas. Night falls.

**868–95** This is one of the most powerful passages in book XI, marked by the frequent deployment of assonance, alliteration and other figures, noted in detail below. For the panic following C.'s death cf. Quintus Smyrnaeus 1.630–42 (panic on the death of Penthesilea)

**868–9 fugit ... fugiunt ... fugit:** for the anaphora cf. 818n.

**870** A striking four-word line, further marked by alliteration and homoeoteleuton (juxtaposition of similar case-endings). Cf. 700n., 8.263 *abstractaeque boues abiurataeque rapinae*, *Georg.* 1.470 *obscenaeque canes importunaeque uolucres*. Hesiod was the first poet to write four-word hexameters, a hallmark of his style imitated by the Alexandrians. V.'s alliterative symmetry, however, represents a further development of the mannerism.

**871 tuta:** neut. pl adj. as substantive: see also 882n.

**872** For the structure of this line cf. 854n.; here there is assonance rather than rhyme between the two participles, and no elision. See also 886–7.

**instantis:** the intrans. usage is common in the Augustans: cf. Hor. *C.* 3.3.3 *uultus instantis tyranni*.

**873 sustentare ... sistere:** this kind of word-play is equally characteristic of Latin and English poetry.

**875** A famous example of onomatopoeia produced by a sequence of dactyls (though the verse is not wholly dactylic, unlike 8.596, of which it is a variant), interlaced alliteration ($q, p, q, p, q, p$) and repeated vowels ($a, u$). V. is imitating Ennius' phrase *summo sonitu quatit ungula terram* (*Ann.* 263; cf. 242, 431). The alliteration of *p* is continued in vv. 877, 879.

**877 percussae pectora:** cf. 35n.

**882 tuta domorum** 'the safe refuge of their homes'. Cf. 2.332 *angusta uiarum*, 2.725 *opaca locorum*, *Georg.* 4.159 *saepta domorum*.

**883–90 pars ... pars:** this collective noun can take a singular or plural verb, or the 'historic' infinitive of repeated or characteristic action. Cf. 1.423–5 (infin.) and Austin's n., 7.624–7 (singular and plural verbs). Here both constructions are used in a characteristic ex. of Virgilian variation. Page, however, suggested that *claudere* might have been attracted by the two other infinitives governed by *audent*, and that we should supply some verb such as *properant* (the figure called zeugma).

**885–6** For the structure of these lines, and the chiastic symmetry of 886 (here given further emphasis by the repeated *armis ... arma*) cf. 12.409–10 *it tristis ad aethera clamor | bellantum iuuenum et duro sub Marte cadentum.* For the homoeoteleuton *defendentum ... ruentum* cf. Palmer 117: it is here strikingly continued into the following line. Pairs of rhymed couplets are not so unusual in V.: the present couplet should be added to the list given by Austin, n. on 4.55. The celebrated ex. at *Ecl.* 4.50–1 (*mundum | ... profundum*) may suggest that such 'jingles' were a feature of Sibylline oracular verses and perhaps of native Latin poetry: cf. Mackail lxxviii.

**885 orantis, oriturque:** for this kind of word-play, which exploits contrasts in metrical quantities, and of which V. is particularly fond, cf. 2.494 *fit uia ui*, 4.238 *ille patris magni parere parabat | imperio*, 8.441 *uiro. nunc uiribus.*

**oriturque miserrima caedes:** repeated from 4.211.

**888 ruina** echoes *ruentum* above.

**890 arietat ... obice:** both are scanned as dactyls (cf. 667n.).

**arietat** 'rams': only here in V.

**duros obice postis** 'strongly-barred gates': an ex. of a characteristically Virgilian use of the abl. with an adjective attached to another noun to produce a 'quasi-adjectival phrase' (Mackail App. A.4).

**892** 'True love of country showed them the way, as they had seen [the example of] Camilla.' A difficult line, on which see Arrigoni 118–23. Servius was surely right to point out that it was the example of C.'s *aristeia* which inspired the matrons: so too in Quintus Smyrnaeus 1.421ff., where the Trojan Tisiphone, inspired by the *aristeia* of Penthesilea, calls on the women of Troy to fight (Quintus Smyrnaeus 1.436–9 corresponds to *Aen.* 11.893–5). In Quintus' narrative Penthesilea is still alive, however; in V.'s narrative, C. lives on through her example. Some commentators have taken *ut uidere Camillam* literally, to mean 'when they saw her body'. V. does not record the carrying away of her body for burial, which Diana had promised to perform *after* the death of her slayer (593 *post ego* ...); it would presumably have still been visible at 834–5, and Sabbadini suggested that 891–5 should be transposed after 835.

The passage from Quintus also throws light on the phrase *uerus amor patriae*: Tisiphone reminds the women of Troy that Penthesilea was not fighting for her own country but for the love of glory: so too, in V.'s narrative the Rutulian women are given a lesson in patriotism by the Volscian Camilla.

**893–4 robore duro | stipitibus** 'with stakes made of tough oak': ablative 'of origin', to be distinguished from the constr. at 890, where the adj. is transferred from the abl. to the other noun.

**896–7** 'Meanwhile the tragic tidings came pouring in to Turnus [as he lay waiting] in the woods, and Acca brought him the dreadful disaster.' For the narrative transition *interea* cf. 532n.; for *implet* cf. 5.341 and a similar use of *replet* at 140, 4.189. The two lines are a good ex. of 'theme and variation'.

**898–900** For the accus. and infin. of *oratio obliqua* after *nuntius* cf. 449–50.

**901 furens:** T.'s *uiolentia* breaks out afresh at the news of C.'s death; *saeua* echoes *saeuissimus* above: Jupiter's will is indeed bitter for T. We sense in this line, which Servius understood correctly, how Turnus' impetuosity and the implacable will of Jupiter together conspire to protect Aeneas. See also 910.

**902** A chiastically symmetrical line.

**903 conspectu exierat:** for the elision of a long vowel at the 3rd-foot caesura see Soubiran 311–15. Elision of *u* is rare: cf. 9.606.

**903–5** Aeneas passes safely through the woods to reach the ridge and the path back to his camp. 'Here the conjunction of the pluperfect and imperfect brings out neatly the "near-miss" quality of Turnus' departure and its folly. When it is just too late – when Turnus has already left and is in the plain – Aeneas with the greatest ease (present tense) sails through the abandoned ambush' (Sara Mack, *Patterns of time in Vergil* (Hamden, Conn. 1978) 47).

This is Aen.'s first appearance in the narrative since the funeral scenes at the beginning of the book.

**908 simul** 'at the same time': the two leaders become simultaneously aware of their closeness to each other.

**910 saeuum:** the repeated word (see 896, 901) sounds out ominously as the book draws to its close, preparing us for book XII: Aen. is again *saeuus* when he reappears at 12.107, as indeed he had been in book X (cf. 10.802, 10.813–14).

**912–14** For the graphic present subjunctives describing a past unfulfilled condition cf. 6.292–4 *at ni docta comes tenuis sine corpore uitas | admoneat uolitare caua sub imagine formae, | inruat et frustra ferro diuerberet umbras.*

For the motif of nightfall preventing further fighting cf. *Il.* 8.485–8 (VIII is the so-called 'Unfinished Battle' book) which ends with Hector elated by Trojan success; *Aen.* XI ends with the Trojans victorious over Camilla and the Rutuli in disarray.

Book XI began with a dawn-formula; the sunset-formula rounds it off.

**gurgite … Hibero:** the Spanish (i.e. western) sea.

**equos:** for the sun's horses cf. 6.535 *roseis Aurora quadrigis*, 12.114–15 *cum primum alto se gurgite tollunt | Solis equi …*

# BIBLIOGRAPHY

This list consists chiefly of works cited in the Introduction and Commentary by the name of author or editor alone. In a few cases, to avoid ambiguity, an abbreviated title has been used. References to 'Williams' are to his complete edition of the *Aeneid*, except for books III and V, where the references are to his separate editions of these books. All references to Ennius' *Annals* are given in Skutsch's numbering. Further bibliographical references will be found at the relevant points in the Commentary and in the notes to the Introduction.

## I. EDITIONS AND COMMENTARIES

Austin, R. G. *Aeneid I* (Oxford 1971).
    *Aeneid II* (Oxford 1964).
    *Aeneid IV* (Oxford 1955).
    *Aeneid VI* (Oxford 1977).
Conington, J., and Nettleship, H. *Works of Virgil*, 3 vols. (London 1858–83).
Conway, R. S. *Aeneid I* (Cambridge 1935).
Fordyce, C. J. *Aeneid VII and VIII* (Oxford 1977).
Fowler, W. W. *Virgil's gathering of the clans: being observations on Aeneid VII, 601–817* (Oxford 1918).
Gransden, K. W. *Aeneid VIII* (Cambridge 1976).
Henry, J. *Aeneidea*, 4 vols. (London – Dublin 1873–92).
Mackail, J. W. *The Aeneid of Virgil* (Oxford 1930).
Norden, E. *Aeneis Buch VI*, 3rd edn (Leipzig 1927, repr. 1957).
Page, T. E. *The Aeneid*. 2 vols. (London 1894–1900).
Paratore, E. *Eneide*, Vol. VI: books XI–XII (Milan 1983).
Servius. *Commentary*, edd. G. Thilo and H. Hagen, 3 vols. (Leipzig 1878–1902).
Tilly, B. *The Story of Camilla*. Edited from books VII and XI, with illustrations and brief notes (Cambridge 1956).
    *The Story of Pallas*. Edited from books VIII, X, XI and XII, with illustrations and brief notes (Cambridge 1961).
Williams, R. D. *The Aeneid of Virgil*, 2 vols. (London 1973).
    *Aeneid III* (Oxford 1962).
    *Aeneid V* (Oxford 1960).

## 2. OTHER WORKS

Alföldi, A. *Early Rome and the Latins* (Ann Arbor 1965).

Allen, W. S. *Accent and rhythm: prosodic features of Latin and Greek* (Cambridge 1973).

Arrigoni, G. *Camilla: Amazone e sacerdotessa di Diana* (Milan 1982).

Bonfanti, M. *Punto di vista e modi della narrazione nell'Eneide* (Pisa 1985).

Büchner, K. *Publius Vergilius Maro: der Dichter der Römer* (Stuttgart 1955).

Camps, W. A. *An introduction to Virgil's Aeneid* (Cambridge 1969).

Cartault, A. *L'Art de Virgile dans l'Eneide* (Paris 1926).

Clausen, W. *Virgil's Aeneid and Hellenistic poetry* (Los Angeles – London 1987).

Coleiro, E. *Tematica e struttura dell' Eneide de Virgilio* (Amsterdam 1983).

Cordier, A. *Etudes sur le vocabulaire épique dans l'Eneide* (Paris 1939).

Cruttwell, R. W. *Virgil's mind at work* (Oxford 1946).

Dilke, C. A. W. 'Do line-totals in the *Aeneid* show a preoccupation with significant number?', *C.Q.* n.s. 17 (1967) 322–7.

*Enciclopedia Virgiliana* i–iv, ed. Umberto Cozzoli (Rome: Istituto dell' enciclopedia Italiana, 1984–   ). (*EV*)

Galinsky, G. K. *Aeneas, Sicily and Rome* (Princeton 1969).

Glare, P. G. W. (ed.) *Oxford Latin Dictionary* (Oxford 1982). (*OLD*)

Gransden, K. W. *Virgil's Iliad* (Cambridge 1984). (*VI*)
   *Virgil's Aeneid* (Landmarks of World Literature, Cambridge 1990). (*VA*)

Grant, M. *Roman myths* (London 1971).

Guillemin, A. M. *Virgile: poète, artiste et penseur* (Paris 1951).

Hardie, P. *Virgil's Aeneid: cosmos and imperium* (Oxford 1986).

Heinze, R. *Virgils epische Technik* (Leipzig, 1928; repr. 1957).

Hellegouarc'h, J. *Le Monosyllabe dans l'hexamètre latin: essai de métrique verbale* (Paris 1964).

Highet, G. *The speeches in Virgil's Aeneid* (Princeton 1972).

Hofmann, J. B. and Szantyr, A. *Lateinische Syntax und Stilistik* (Munich 1965).

Johnson, W. R. *Darkness visible* (Los Angeles – London 1976).

Klingner, F. *Virgil: Bucolica, Georgica, Aeneis* (Zurich – Stuttgart 1967).

Knauer, G. *Die Aeneis und Homer* (Göttingen 1964).

Lyne, R. O. A. M. 'Virgil and the politics of war', *C.Q.* n.s. 33 (1983) 188–203.

Marouzeau, J. *Traité de stylistique latine* (Paris 1946).

Newman, J. K. *Augustus and the new poetry* (Brussels 1967).

*The Classical epic tradition* (Wisconsin 1986). (*CET*)

Ogilvie, R. M. *Early Rome and the Etruscans* (London 1976).

Otis, B. *Virgil: a study in civilised poetry* (Oxford 1964).

Ott, W. *Rückläufiger Wortindex zu Vergil* (Tübingen 1974).

Palmer, L. R. *The Latin language* (London 1954).

Pearce, T. E. V. 'Enclosing word-order in the Latin hexameter', *C.Q.* n.s. 16 (1966) 140–71, 298–320.

Pöschl, V. *Die Dichtkunst Virgils: Bild und symbol in der Aeneis* (Berlin – New York 1977). Translated as *The art of Virgil* by G. Seligson (Ann Arbor 1962).

Putnam, M. J. C. *The poetry of the Aeneid* (Cambridge, Mass. 1965).

Quinn, K. *Virgil's Aeneid: a critical description* (London 1969).

*Latin explorations* (London 1963). (*LE*)

Schlunk, R. B. *The Homeric scholia and the Aeneid* (Ann Arbor 1974).

Schweitzer, H. J. *Vergil und Italien* (Aarau 1967).

Silk, M. *Homer: the Iliad* (Cambridge 1987).

Skutsch, O. *The Annals of Q. Ennius* (Oxford 1985).

Soubiran, J. *L'Elision dans la poésie latine* (Paris 1966).

Wigodsky, M. *Vergil and early Latin poetry.* Hermes: Zeitschrift für Klassische Philologie. Einzelschriften 24. (Wiesbaden 1972)

Wilkinson, L. P. *Golden Latin artistry* (Cambridge 1963).

Williams, G. *Tradition and originality in Roman poetry* (Oxford 1968). (*TORP*)

*Techniques and ideas in the Aeneid* (New Haven – London 1983). (*TIA*)

Włosok, A. *Die Göttin Venus in Vergils Aeneis* (Heidelberg 1967).

# INDEXES

*References are to lines of the text.*

## I LATIN WORDS

*adeo*, 275–6, 314, 369, 436
*aequo*, 125
*aequus*, 115
*arduus*, 755
*atque*, 182–3, 668, 725

*captiuus*, 779
*caput*, 361
*cassus*, 104
*copia*, 248, 378
*corona*, 475

*de* (elliptical), 15
*decurro*, 189
*defleo*, 59
*denseo*, 650
*dia*, 657
*discrimino*, 144
*dulcedo*, 538

*ecce*, 448, 547
*ei mihi*, 57
*Eous*, 4
*equidem*, 111
*et* ( = 'as'), 87, 784
*et* (postponed), 367

*fama*, 139
*farier* ( = *fari*), 242
*fatalis*, 112, 130, 232
*fors*, 50
*fragor*, 214
*fraus*, 708, 717

*gloria*, 708

*hic* (deictic), 16, 115, 127
*heu nimium*, 841

*ille* (deictic), 257, 494, 809
*immo*, 459
*immugio*, 38
*importunus*, 305
*improbus*, 512
*ingrauo*, 220
*iniquus*, 531
*insignio*, 386
*interea*, 1, 532, 597
*intersum*, 62
*inuisus*, 364
*is*, 12
*iste*, 165–6, 390, 409, 537–8
*iusso* (archaic fut. perf.), 467

*labor*, 183
*lustro*, 190

*maestus*, 26, 482
*manu*, 116, 453, 505, 650, 817
*Mars* (*Mauors*), 374, 389
*Mors*, 197
*mulco*, 839
*musso*, 345, 454

*nec non*, 477, 603

*obumbro*, 223
*olli*, 236
*oppetio*, 268
*orator*, 100, 331

*pars*, 193–6, 883–90
*potis est* ( = *potest*), 148
*praediues*, 213
*praedo*, 484
*praesto*, 438
*premo*, 402

## 2 GENERAL

Illiad ends with human understanding
(Achilles giving Hectors' body back
to Prian )

Aeneid ends with Aeneas killing Turnus

The Etruscan city is the future site of
Rome — funeral procession going to Rome